Cardinals Glory

Cardinals Glory

FOR THE LOVE OF DIZZY, OZZIE, AND THE MAN

ALAN ROSS

Cumberland House
Nashville, Tennessee

Published by
Cumberland House Publishing, Inc.
431 Harding Industrial Drive
Nashville, TN 37211-3160

Cover design: Gore Studio, Inc., Nashville, Tennessee
Book design: John Mitchell
Research assistant: Andrew Gearing Ross

Library of Congress Cataloging-in-Publication Data

Ross, Alan, 1944–
  Cardinals glory : for the love of Dizzy, Ozzie, and The Man / Alan Ross.
  p. cm.
  Includes bibliographical references and index.
  ISBN 1-58182-446-7 (pbk. : alk. paper)
  1. St. Louis Cardinals (Baseball team)—History. I. Title.
  GV875.S4R67 2005
                                2004030481

Printed in Canada
1 2 3 4 5 6 7—11 10 09 08 07 06 05

For Andrew Gearing,
thanks for your dedicated assistance
but especially for your wonderful humor,
keen mind, restful soul . . .
and other "Cardinal sins"

and for Caroline,
my true love and ever-inspirational
life partner, who more than ever
appreciates the wonder of Dizzy Dean

Stan Musial early in his career with St. Louis.

CONTENTS

INTRODUCTION

IT MAY HAVE TAKEN the St. Louis Cardinals a while to get rolling (they didn't gain their first World Series crown until their 35th year of play, in 1926), but they've more than made up for it since, today ranking only behind the mighty New York Yankees in number of world championships, with nine.

Through the years, the Gateway City has been host to both stirring and sterling baseball: the Hornsby-Bottomley-Alexander teams of the mid-1920s; the gritty, audacious Gas House Gang of the '30s, spearheaded by the legendary Dizzy Dean; the smooth and efficient Cardinals of the Musial-Slaughter-Cooper brothers era that took home three world crowns; the Gibson-Brock-Boyer days of the '60s; "Whiteyball" in the '80s, and currently, Tony La Russa's power-hitting Redbirds of the late 1990s through the 2004 National League pennant winners.

Cardinals Glory is the story of the National League's St. Louis franchise, as told by the players themselves, the managers, the coaches, opponents, fans, and members of the media. An all-time Cardinals nine is presented, as well as the complete rosters of all the world champion Cardinals teams, a chapter on the various St. Louis venues, the storied rivalries, and even a shrine of superlatives to the greatest Cardinal of them all—Stan Musial.

From Rogers to Red, Dizzy to Ozzie, Musial to McGee, and Pepper to Pujols—it's consummate birds on the bat.

REMEMBRANCE

A GAME AGAINST THE archrival Cubs, a one-hitter, back-to-back St. Louis home runs in the first inning, an unusual triple play, a major-league-leading stolen base, and a Redbirds victory—not bad for a first time at a Cardinals game.

That inaugural trek, on Aug. 8, 1985, began with obligatory reverence at the shrine—the compelling bronze statue of Baseball's Perfect Knight: The Man, Stan Musial, on the stadium plaza.

Play was resuming that night, after the second players' strike in five years had abruptly terminated after just two days. Welcoming baseball back to Busch were 39,203 fans, who doubtless felt fortunate they weren't having to sit through a possible cancellation of the season's final two months. And what a treat was in store for us.

Throughout that muggy August evening, I tried soaking up the storied Cardinal Red ambience. The arches were a stadium treatment that I found appealing back when I first saw pictures of the facility in the mid-sixties. In late afternoon, sunlight creates a shadow mosaic not seen at any other venue.

As for action, I didn't have to wait long. In the bottom of the first, St. Louis jumped on Chicago starter Scott Sanderson for five runs, including Andy Van Slyke's and Terry Pendleton's back-to-back homers. Staff ace John Tudor earned his 14th victory of the season, the 13th win in his last 14 starts, a sparkling one-hitter against the arch-foe Cubs. The southpaw even laced a triple in his complete-game performance. It was a happy throng that took in that 8–0 Cardinals win, witnessing Vince Coleman's major-league-leading 75th stolen base plus a strange triple play in the eighth involving two Cardinals, Van Slyke and Jack Clark, both getting caught in rundowns after a line-drive infield out by Pendleton.

While contemporary times have brought a flock of new Redbird stars to Busch, for me the St. Louis Cardinals will always be embodied in that classic coiled stance of No. 6 at the plate, Stan Musial. Growing up in the late 1940s and early '50s, it seemed the St. Louis star was in every issue of *SPORT* magazine that I leafed through. I once had the Tom Meany book on The Man that was part of a children's series, since slipped through my grasp and now a valued collector's item.

The once-westernmost outpost of major-league baseball now ranks second only to the Yankees in world crowns. Though 2004 ended with a rude shock, things bode well in Redbirdland. For certain, those birds on the bat are in a chirping frenzy.

— A.R.

CARDINAL
TRADITION

HERE, TRADITION IS STAN Musial and Bob Gibson and Lou Brock walking into the clubhouse. In San Diego, it was [former Padres star] Nate Colbert trying to sell you a used car.

Bob Shirley
pitcher (1981)

It's the Cardinal Way. It's the way the Gas House Gang went about its business. It's the feisty Orlando Cepeda-led "El Birdos" of 1967. It's Whiteyball. It's Slaughter crying after being told he no longer would wear the birds on the bat—he had just been traded to the Yankees. It is tradition.

Rob Rains
author

St. Louis representation in the National League goes all the way back to 1876, the nation's centennial and the year the old National was born. Though a charter member, St. Louis's sojourn in the league has not been continuous. There were two breaks: from 1878 to 1884, and 1887 to 1891.

Frederick G. Lieb
*legendary sports
journalist/author*

The present Cardinal club actually is the direct lineal offspring of the American Association Browns of the 1880s, rather than of the St. Louis National League clubs of 1876–77 and 1885–86.

Frederick G. Lieb

When baseball season starts in St. Louis, they bleed Cardinal Red.

Mark McGwire
first baseman (1997–2001)

The Cardinals' name emerged as a result of a female fan being astounded by the bright red caps and socks of the players. The remark was within earshot of local sportswriter Willie McHale, who made the suggestion for the team name in his column the following day.

Doug Feldmann
author

That colorful, picturesque word, *Cardinals*, goes back to 1899, when Willie McHale, then a cub St. Louis baseball writer, suggested it in his column in the old *St. Louis Republic*. St. Louis National League clubs then were the Browns, and Willie thought some of the brownish taste of years of second-division baseball might disappear with a new, more vivid nickname.

Frederick G. Lieb

She was an early advocate of "Ladies Day" many years before the idea became popular among baseball promoters. Mrs. Britton felt that "We just have to prevail upon more members of the fair sex to come out and see the Cardinals play!"

Bill Borst
author,
on 1916 Cardinals owner
Helene "Lady Bee" Britton

Chris Von der Ahe was baseball's early-day Bill Veeck/Ray Dumont/Larry McPhail —an innovator-promoter. Chris put a "chute the chutes" carnival ride, an early-day water slide in which patrons boarded boats atop a large tower for a wet trip down the slide into a man-made lake below. Just beyond the left-field fence, a beer garden, night horse racing, boating, boxing, a Wild West show, and an all-girls Silver Coronet Band rounded out the amusements.

Bob Broeg
longtime St. Louis Post-Dispatch *sports editor/author, on the early Cardinals owner (1892–97)*

Von der Ahe called his amusement conglomerate the "Coney Island of the West."

Here we play baseball as "it oughta be." And that tradition exists generation after generation in St. Louis.

John W. Maher
fan

For many years, the Cardinals were the westernmost and southernmost major-league team, and evidence of their fan base was seen in a great radius. Through the later 1930s, '40s, '50s, and into the '60s, a game broadcast on the powerful KMOX station in St. Louis reached the deepest corners of the country. A barber shop in Mississippi, a restaurant in Memphis, a gas station in Joplin—all had attentive ears lurking on the premises.

Doug Feldmann

The revolutionary farm system itself is a key component of the Cardinals' rich history—and success. Created by Branch Rickey in the 1920s, it put the Cards far ahead of other teams in the signing and development of talent. The farm chain had as many as 25 teams at one point.

Rob Rains

Starting the Cardinal farm system was no sudden stroke of genius. It was a case of necessity being the mother of invention. We lived a precarious existence. We would trade one player for four, and then maybe sell one who developed for a little extra cash with which to buy a few minor-leaguers others passed up.

Branch Rickey

president (1917–19)/
manager (1919–25)/
general manager (1917–42)

The golden years of the St. Louis Cardinals arrived when Sam Breadon, "Mr. Red Bird," took over active management of the flagging baseball team. During his 28 seasons as an active participant, the Cardinals won nine pennants and six World Series. From 1920 until his forced retirement in 1947, when he sold the ball club to Fred Saigh and Bob Hannegan, his team finished in the first division 22 times, a remarkable feat in any sport.

Bill Borst

After the way the fans flocked to see them play, I'll never again be afraid to trade a star.

Sam Breadon

owner (1920–47),
who experienced resounding
criticism from fans after trading
Rogers Hornsby the winter
following the Cardinals' first-ever
world championship, in 1926

Rickey and his business associate in St. Louis, Sam Breadon, have been accused of being "tight" when it came to paying players' salaries. I don't subscribe to that at all. Those were struggling days for ball clubs. There was no night baseball, crowds were small, and the baseball operators had to be shrewd businessmen. And the Cardinals didn't pay salaries any lower than were paid in other cities.

Frankie Frisch
*second baseman (1927–37)/
manager (1933–38)*

In terms of encompassing an entire region, the Cardinals' following is unparalleled. This status was recognized by St. Louis being named as the "Best Baseball City" by *Baseball America* magazine in 1998.

Doug Feldmann

In the morning edition of the *New York Telegraph* on Oct. 9, 1934, a peculiar cartoon appeared. Sportswriter Dan Daniel described some rough-looking ballplayers with their cleats slung over their shoulders, crossing the railroad tracks to the "nice" part of town to play the "nice" team. The rough team, depicted as the Cardinals, was labeled as "the Gas House Gang," coming from the tough gashouse district of town. Little did Mr. Daniel know at the time that the moniker would be forever linked with the most hard-nosed team in the history of American sports.

Doug Feldmann

August Busch riding into his stadium before league playoff or World Series games in a wagon drawn by an eight-horse hitch of Clydesdales, waving his red cowboy hat to the cheers of the crowd, had become part of the legend of St. Louis baseball.

Donald Honig

author/historian

As is St. Louis tradition, another generation will hear the roll call. They will hear about the men who wore the uniform and played hard and never forgot the people who loved them, the fans who supported them when they were down and cheered them in victory. The game will live on in St. Louis. And that's baseball like it oughta be.

John W. Maher

I understand that times have changed, ballparks have changed. But if you look back, the only times the Cardinals have had great teams, it's been run, run, run. From the Gas House team of the 1930s to the teams of the '80s, when the Cardinals had great teams, it seems like they always had an aggressive leadoff hitter and a great stopper. You don't want to lose that aggressive, Cardinal way of playing baseball. That's the tradition. That's the legacy.

Bob Forsch
pitcher (1974–88)

Through it all, those two redbirds on the front of those St. Louis uniforms have remained poised and steadfast, as though always absolutely confident of victory.

Donald Honig

2

CARDINAL RED

*N*OT EVERY PLAYER WITH *major-league talent can be like Stan, Red, or Gibby; Mark, Ozzie, or Albert. The everyday working fabric of Cardinals baseball is supported just as importantly by timely contributions from a Lonnie Smith, a Wilmer "Vinegar Bend" Mizell, or a Dal Maxvill. Some almost reach the heights of Cooperstown: the Marions, Boyers, Simmonses, Torres, Hernandezes, and McGees. Each with their unique contribution, all in Cardinal Red.*

If I was manager and I wanted one ball game that meant the pennant or World Series, I would rather have Bill Hallahan pitching than any of them. He was wild, but if he got the ball over the plate, they didn't beat him too often.

Spud Davis

catcher (1928, 1934–36),
on the Cardinals' mound ace
of 1925–26 and 1929–36

The first big-league infielder to wear glasses on the field was George Toporcer [1921–28], who backed up at third, short, and second for the Cardinals. Inevitably, they called him "Specs." A .324 average in 1933 was his best.

Donald Honig

The flamboyant Pepper Martin hustled his way into baseball history with an extraordinary World Series [in 1931]. He had 12 hits—the official scorer denied him a thirteenth by giving Jimmie Foxx an error on the play—and five stolen bases. In Game 5, a 5–1 win, Martin had a home run and two singles and drove in four of the runs. He handled 10 balls in center without an error. By the end of the Series, Martin had gained immortality with his spirited play. Though he was from Oklahoma, his nickname was "the Wild Horse of the Osage," an area that is in Arkansas.

Peter Golenbock
author

Pepper Martin

The Cardinals' great Pepper Martin, the folks back home in Temple, Oklahoma, said, "was so fast that he spent his boyhood chasing down rabbits."

Doug Feldmann

Pepper goes out on the prairie and scares up a bunch of rabbits. He runs along with these rabbits and reaches down and feels their sides. If the rabbit is a bit thin, he lets him go.

Roy Moore

major-league pitcher with Philadelphia and Detroit (1920–23), who knew Martin in the minors in the late 1920s

Pepper was plain folks. He was not braggadocious, but rather confident. He had a wonderful arm.

Gene Karst

Cardinals' first director of publicity (1931–33)

Pepper was a mess, you know. He didn't wear underwear or a jockstrap. Everything with Pepper was awkward. He would try to hit the ball to left, and he'd hit a line drive to right. If he was playing in the outfield, I'd see him run in to get down on one knee and catch the ball cross-handed, and it looked like he would catch the ball with his bare hand. Pepper was a good ballplayer, just awkward. He'd run to first base real hard and he'd stop, instead of running through the play and slowing down. I'd think, "Jeez, you're going to tear your knee ligaments."

Bob Broeg

Nobody could figure Martin out, nor predict what he would do next. He was a strongly built, fireplug of a man. He played the harmonica in the clubhouse, loved to eat his mother's home cooking back in Oklahoma, and hunted rattlesnakes for the St. Louis Zoo in the off-season, arming himself with only a forked stick and a canvas bag.

Doug Feldmann

People talk about Cool Papa Bell in the Negro Leagues, and he was pretty quick, for sure, but he was no match for Martin. Pepper was by far the fastest man in the game. And he would outrun any of the modern players today.

Mickey Owen
catcher (1937–40)

Once we had three guys chasing him around in a rundown, and we were the ones who felt surrounded.

Anonymous National League infielder

on Pepper Martin

The best thing a manager could have is nine Pepper Martins on the field.

Frankie Frisch

Look at them! There is [Wild Bill] Hallahan of cyclonic velocity; the venerable [Jesse] Haines, wise as a serpent; and that battle-scarred warrior, home again from the foreign legions, the Tamerlane of the diamond, Burleigh Grimes himself.

Anonymous editorial writer

St. Louis Post-Dispatch,
spring 1934,
on the veteran pitching staff supporting the fabulous Dean brothers

Paul Dean will be another Walter Johnson.

Sid Keener

St. Louis Star Times

The farm system sent up Terry Moore in 1935; he would soon have a reputation as a peerless defensive center fielder, with an arm so strong infielders said his pegs came in like cannon shots and "hurt."

Donald Honig

I've said it before and I'll say it again: Defensively, he is, without a doubt, the greatest center fielder I ever played alongside. For that matter, he was the best I've ever seen.

Enos Slaughter

on Terry Moore (1935–42, 1946–48)

Marty Marion was not a flamboyant player of high and lofty tumbling or low and fancy diving but performed his mastery on the infield in a slow, methodical, smooth, and businesslike manner in establishing control of the game through his presence on the field.

Bill Borst

A quiet, unassuming man who looked upon his talent in modest terms, "the Octopus" had great cruising range at his position despite a chronically sore back. His fielding was often compared to that of Honus Wagner, reputed to be the game's greatest shortstop. This earned Marion the sobriquet of "Mr. Shortstop."

Bill Borst

Of course Honus was a better hitter, but I don't think he could cover more ground than Marty Marion.

Connie Mack

Hall of Fame manager-owner
of the Philadelphia Athletics

At the end of the 1936 season, the club brought up minor-league first baseman Walter Alston for a sip of coffee. The 24-year-old had one at-bat, struck out, and then returned to the minor leagues, where he would play and manage until 1954, when he resurfaced to begin a 23-year career as manager of the Brooklyn and Los Angeles Dodgers.

Donald Honig

He gained fame as a broadcaster in part by poking fun at his playing ability. In fact, he was a decent player. As a 20-year-old Cards rookie, Joe Garagiola batted .316 in the 1946 World Series and had four hits in Game 4.

Rob Rains

I wish you were twins.

Eddie Dyer

*manager (1946–50),
to Harry "the Cat" Brecheen,
winner of three games in the
1946 World Series triumph
over Boston*

He can't run, he can't throw, he can't hit. He can only beat you.

Branch Rickey

*on second baseman (1952–53)
and future Cardinals manager
(1952–55) Eddie Stanky*

Harry Caray nicknamed Mizell "Vinegar Bend" after Wilmer's hometown in Alabama. Harry always claimed it was his favorite baseball player hometown.

Raymond Warfel

fan

The high-kicking Mizell (1952–53, 1956–60), later a North Carolina congressman, still ranks ninth all-time among Cardinal pitchers in strikeouts.

Von McDaniel was 7–5 for the 1957 Cardinals as an 18-year-old direct out of high school, including a two-hit shutout over Brooklyn in his first major-league start. He pitched in two games in 1958, hurt his arm and saw his career over at age 19.

Rob Rains

When Lindy McDaniel and younger brother Von made a sensational splash in the mid-1950s, Cardinals fans may have thought they were seeing the reincarnation of Dizzy and Paul Dean. Like both Dean brothers, Von, a supernova, burned brilliantly but briefly, exiting even quicker than the Deans with career-ending arm problems. Lindy, though, went on to have a 21-year major-league career, the first eight with St. Louis.

Ken Boyer

Ken Boyer wasn't the fastest player ever to play for the Cardinals, but he did something not many players have accomplished. In a three-week span in 1959, Boyer hit three inside-the-park home runs.

Rob Rains

Ken was my idol. He could run, he could throw, he could hit, and he could think. He was a quiet leader. If we changed places and Ken played in New York, he'd be in the Hall of Fame today.

Cletis Boyer
New York Yankees third baseman (1959–66),
on brother Ken

Tim McCarver was becoming recognized as the best catcher in the National League, both offensively and defensively. He had a low strikeout total because he didn't swing at bad pitches. In 1966, he was the fifth toughest to fan in the league. McCarver reminded people of Mickey Cochrane with his aggressiveness and speed.

Mel Freese
author

Tim had an uncanny way with pitchers. A lot of catchers are just putting down fingers. Not Tim. He was always thinking. He remembered the sequences of pitches we used to get a hitter out. He had great instincts.

Steve Carlton
*Hall of Fame pitcher (1965–71),
on Tim McCarver*

In Dal Maxvill we had a shortstop who wasn't a great hitter, but he always seemed to come up with big hits at big times. He knew how to win, that was his biggest attribute. He made the big plays at the critical moments in games. You see a lot of players make plays when their team either is getting beat by a big margin or way ahead, but the players I wanted on my team were the ones who could make the big plays when the game was tied or a one- or two-run margin. Maxie was that kind of player. You won with guys like that on your team.

Red Schoendienst

second baseman (1945–56, 1961–63)/manager (1965–76, 1980, 1990),
on the Cardinals shortstop/ second baseman from 1962–72

He was called "the Phantom" because he got out of the way [making a double play] so quickly that no runner could slide into him. He just disappeared.

Jack Buck

on Julian Javier,
second baseman (1960–71)

The hitters go to Groat and they say, "How do you do this?" And the pitchers go to him and they say, "Hey Dick, how was I throwing today?" He knows the answers because he has made it his business to know them. He thinks about this game.

Ken Boyer

on the Redbirds' two-time All-Star
shortstop from 1963–65

Maybe there were better hitters than this lefty with the grooved swing, and better outfielders and faster runners. But Roger was a complete player, modest to a fault, and an honest if not particularly warm fellow.

Maury Allen
longtime New York Post
columnist/author
on right fielder Roger Maris
(1967–68)

Trading Orlando Cepeda to the Braves for Joe Torre had been a good deal. Joe knew how to play, and he played hard. He was the type of player who you could tell was hoping to stay in the game after his playing career was over, and that was one of the reasons he paid close attention to what was going on, trying to soak up all of the knowledge that he could.

Red Schoendienst

We acquired Richie Allen in the Flood trade, and he was a good player for the Cardinals. It was hard for right-handed hitters at that time to hit the ball to right-center with any authority, and he could do it. He had a reputation of being a difficult player, but he played hard for me. The only problem I had with him, and it was true throughout his career, is that he never seemed to play the last month of the season. He was always hurt or something was wrong.

Red Schoendienst

Allen batted in 101 runs and slugged 34 home runs, hitting .279 in his only season, 1970, with St. Louis.

The "Mad Hungarian" was entertaining even before throwing a pitch, psyching himself up near the mound then storming to the rubber to face a hitter. He was at his dramatic best in a national-TV game on the night of May 9, 1977, when he struck out the Reds' George Foster, Johnny Bench, and Bob Bailey with the bases full in the ninth inning of a tie game. The Cards won in the 10th.

Rob Rains

on relief pitcher Al Hrabosky
(1970–77)

Darrell Porter lacked Ted Simmons's bat, but he was a highly efficient catcher. He would never regain the glory of his Kansas City Royals days. Nor would he ever be taken into the hearts of the St. Louis fans like Simmons. In replacing Simmons, Whitey Herzog had displaced an excellent hitting catcher who was one of the most popular players on the team.

Mel Freese

He didn't sound like a baseball player. He said things like "Nevertheless" and "If, in fact."

Dan Quisenberry
pitcher (1988–89),
on catcher Ted Simmons

Ted Simmons

Garry Templeton did possess great ability—he had two 200-hit years with the Cardinals, was the first switch hitter in the majors to get 100 hits from each side of the plate in one season, and led the NL in triples three consecutive years. Whitey Herzog always raved about his sheer talent.

Rob Rains

on the Cardinals' shortstop from 1976–81

Bob Forsch earned his spot in club history by becoming the only Cardinals pitcher to throw two no-hitters [vs. the Phillies in 1978, the Expos in 1983]. He was a double-figure winner 10 times for the Cards and ranks third in franchise wins with 163.

Rob Rains

He always impressed me, the way he played in the field, even if he went through a hitting slump. A lot of guys will take their batting problems into the field with them, lose their concentration, and mess up defensively as well. Even if Keith went 0–for–4, he might come up with a play in the field that would help the team win. That's the kind of concentration it takes to be a good player.

Red Schoendienst

on Keith Hernandez,
first baseman (1974–83)

You're my third hitter every game this year. You're the man.

Ken Boyer

third baseman (1955–65)/
manager (1978–80),
to a slumping Keith Hernandez,
batting .232 in April 1979.
Hernandez went on to hit .344,
win the batting title, and share
the NL MVP Award with the
Pirates' Willie Stargell

Willie McGee

Lonnie Smith was another guy who seemed to win no matter where he went in his career. He had desire and he played the game hard. He could break up a double play as well as anybody. He wasn't that great an outfielder and he didn't have a tremendous arm, but when the game was on the line he always seemed to make the play or the throw that needed to be made.

Red Schoendienst

Smith played with St. Louis from 1982 to 1985.

Willie was so unselfish. He did whatever it took to win a game.

Bob Forsch

on center fielder Willie McGee

Willie McGee was always listening, always asking questions, wanting to learn anything he could to become a better player. He went out and worked hard every day on all facets of the game—hitting, defense, baserunning. He likes to play, he likes the game, and that's refreshing. Everything he does on the field, he does hard.

Red Schoendienst

Pitcher Joaquin Andujar said that everything about baseball could be summed up in one word—Youneverknow.

Rob Rains

When I was in the big leagues, I was a big fundamental guy. I moved runners over. I squeezed them in. I played good defense. I've seen a lot of guys who didn't make the major leagues because they didn't know how to play the fundamentals.

Jose Oquendo
infielder (1986–95)/coach (1999–)

What we've been asking for is a starting pitcher to go out and pitch like he did. I think he did a real good job to give us a chance to win. He's shown that a lot—where he doesn't spook with men on base. In fact, he gets tougher a lot of times.

Tony La Russa
manager (1996–),
on pitcher Jason Marquis (2004–)

He starts rallies with singles, doubles. What you see so far in the [2004] post-season, he's had four years of that.

Tony La Russa
on Albert Pujols

It's every little boy's dream. I'm glad to have won the MVP, but that trophy is going to stay right in this room. Because everybody here is MVP.

Albert Pujols
2004 NLCS MVP

The 2001 NL rookie of the year and 2003 NL batting champion, Pujols, only the third player to reach 500 RBIs in his first four seasons, joining Hall of Famers Joe DiMaggio and Ted Williams, is the first player to start his career with four consecutive 30-homer seasons. In spring training 2004, he became the highest-paid player in franchise history with a seven-year, $100 million contract. He went on to hit .331 with 46 homers and 123 RBIs.

CARDINAL CHARACTER

THIS IS A BASEBALL team that is built on a great tradition, one that goes back more than 100 years. When I was a rookie on the 1941 Cardinals, we had a spirit that we knew was greater than any one player. We had an attitude that there was no way we were going to lose, and we didn't.

Stan Musial
*left fielder/right fielder/
first baseman (1941–44,
1946–63)*

I've always worked hard at everything I've done. All you can try to do is work hard every day and get the maximum out of what it is you possess. I think I've done that.

Ozzie Smith
shortstop (1982–96)

Fans have cheered Jose Oquendo and Rex Hudler and Joe McEwing, not because they were great players, but because they played the game at warp speed, diving for balls, sliding headfirst.

Rob Rains

Hate is a good thing, as long as you keep it under control. When it comes out in anger, you lose.

Al "the Mad Hungarian" Hrabosky
relief pitcher (1970–77)

Bob Gibson didn't talk to opponents. He barely talked to his St. Louis teammates on the days he was pitching, and he rarely smiled. Gibson's competitiveness was part of what made him so successful. He once hit a batter in a spring-training game because the player had attempted to bunt. He dusted off former teammates. He glowered.

Rob Rains

On July 13, 1967, in the midst of another strong season, Gibson suffered a broken leg when he was struck by a Roberto Clemente line drive. The gritty right-hander tried to stay in the game, even pitching to another batter before being taken out. It was assumed he would be lost for the season, but Gibson was back in six weeks.

Donald Honig

A St. Louis ball club, because of the city's summer climate wearing down the players, must be 25 percent stronger than any other major-league club to win.

John McGraw

New York Giants manager
(1902–32)

When I played for John McGraw, I was taught to fight to the finish, and you can bet your last dollar that every man playing for me will do the same.

Frankie Frisch

Pepper Martin played with a broken finger, and nobody knew it until he threw the ball across the diamond and yards of bandage came following behind it. When the writers asked him about it after the game, he said, "It's only a small bone."

Doug Feldmann

Pepper Martin plays baseball with a spirit of adventure.

Branch Rickey

The Dean brothers were inseparable. Naturally, Dizzy did all the talking, with the quiet younger brother nodding his agreement. The big change was that the boasts now began "Me 'n' Paul." Dizzy insisted his kid brother was the better pitcher. There was no jealousy between the two young men. Each was genuinely excited by the success of the other.

Jack Kavanagh
author

In '42 we played together and fought together. . . . We had that Cardinal spirit. We thought we could beat anybody, and we did.

Stan Musial

Building fences [as a youth], Red Schoendienst was struck in the eye by a ricocheting nail. Doctors at first feared they would have to remove the eye, but Schoendienst begged them not to take it, saying he was going to be a baseball player. The fact that he worked so hard with eye exercises to overcome the injury was a testament to Schoendienst's work ethic.

Rob Rains

Luck is the residue of design.

Branch Rickey

Branch Rickey's theme was: The greatest attribute of a winning ballplayer is a desire to win that dominates! I have never forgotten those words.

Pepper Martin
third baseman/center fielder
(1928, 1930–40, 1944)

During the month of September, Burleigh Grimes had appendicitis. Doc Hyland would use ice on him. They didn't want to operate during the pennant race. As I remember, he was pitching into the ninth inning of the seventh game [of the 1931 World Series], and he was taking an awful lot of time between pitches. He was obviously in pain, and finally they had to take him out. Bill Hallahan went in and finished the ball game for him.

Gene Karst

When they threw at me, I knew they belonged to me, that they were afraid to pitch to me.

Joe "Ducky" Medwick
left fielder (1932–40, 1947–48)

In Game 3 of the 1982 World Series, he got a line drive back at him that hit off his leg. Dave LaPoint and somebody else went out and carried him off the field. He got the win that game. Then he came back and pitched the seventh game . . . and won it to clinch the world championship.

Bob Forsch

on Joaquin Andujar

I don't believe in hustle, if by hustle you mean always running off and on the field and hollering to make yourself heard. To me, hustle means being alert to take the extra base, putting out 100 percent, doing anything within your power to win. But it doesn't include running the 100-yard dash back and forth from the dugout.

Ken Boyer

I like dirty-suit players, hard-nosed guys like Mike Schmidt, Ken Reitz, and others. You can have those guys who get up and carefully dust themselves off.

Lou Brock
left fielder (1964–79)

You have to find a way to win, and not just with the long ball. You have to hit a bunt, you have to steal a base.

Albert Pujols
first baseman (2001–)

Having mastered what I had once feared, I realized the importance of practice, practice, and more practice.

Enos Slaughter

Initially, Slaughter was fearful of ground balls. During the future Hall of Famer's rookie year, pitcher Lon Warneke, "the Arkansas Hummingbird," spent hours both at home and on the road hitting balls to Slaughter until he was comfortable fielding grounders.

He led by example, and he had that innate ability to make those good players around him even better.

Stan Musial
on Red Schoendienst

Some guys only put out when they know the boss is watching or the camera is running, but not Enos Slaughter. It wasn't a put-on with him. Whatever it took, he was going to win. He played hard all the time.

Red Schoendienst

My players never give up. They are fighters. They don't know when they are licked.

Frankie Frisch

You've got to have an attitude if you're going to go far in this game.

Bob Gibson

CARDINAL HUMOR

A SLICK WAY TO outfigure a person is to get him figuring you figure he's figuring you're figuring he'll figure you aren't really figuring what you want him to figure you figure.

Whitey Herzog
manager (1980–90)

I don't want to play golf. When I hit a ball, I want someone else to go chase it.

Rogers Hornsby
second baseman (1915–26, 1933)/
manager (1925–26)

Your Holiness, I'm Joseph Medwick. I, too, used to be a Cardinal.

Ducky Medwick
when asked by the Pope, during
a World War II visit to the
Vatican by U.S. servicemen,
about his vocation in civilian life

If I'd a-known you was gonna throw one, I'd a-thrown one, too.

Dizzy Dean
pitcher (1930, 1932–37),
to brother Paul, after the latter's
no-hitter against the Dodgers in
the second game of a double-
header, Sept. 21, 1934, at Ebbets
Field. Diz had three-hit Brooklyn
in the opener

Them ain't lies, them is scoops.

Dizzy Dean

on his reason for giving three different birth places to three different reporters. Dean gave out different hometowns and birthdays to oblige each sportswriter with an exclusive interview

That's the only time a team ever lost 30 games in one day.

Jim Lindsey

pitcher (1929–34),
at the conclusion of 1931 spring training, when the Cardinals headed north without Dizzy Dean, electing to season him in the minors one more year

He was always a prankster, once registering in a hotel as gangster Pretty Boy Floyd. The local sheriff wasn't amused.

Rob Rains

on the antics of Dizzy Dean

I won't play for your chain gang.

Leo Durocher
shortstop (1933–37),
to Cardinals GM Branch Rickey,
who had traded for the
Cincinnati Reds shortstop
16 games into the 1933 season

Your reputation doesn't worry me one bit, son. I made this trade because I think the St. Louis ball club can win a lot of pennants with you at shortstop. This deal was made because in my opinion you're just what we need. You can do it for us, you can turn this trick for us, you can make us go, you can be the spark. With you on the team, we can win pennant after pennant after pennant.

Branch Rickey
to Leo Durocher

The more Branch Rickey talks, the smarter and the nicer he becomes. In fact, I'm beginning to become just a little indignant about all the vicious slanders that certain people have been spreading about this brilliant baseball man, this keen judge of talent, this biblical scholar.

Leo Durocher

upon spending time with Rickey, after first declaring he would never play for him

Printed in St. Louis, *The Sporting News* called him "the most dangerous .250 hitter in either league."

Doug Feldmann

on Gas House Gang shortstop Leo Durocher

The Bambino would be the one to later dub Leo Durocher "the All-American Out."

Doug Feldmann

We were watching that ball for two innings.

Jim Lindsey

on Philadelphia Athletics slugger Jimmie Foxx, who, in the fourth game of the 1931 World Series against St. Louis, hit a monster shot over the left-field pavilion

He was so fast, when he went rabbit hunting, he'd outrun the rabbit, overtake it, and reach down and feel how plump it was, before deciding whether to put it in his sack or not.

Branch Rickey

on Pepper Martin

We used basically simple signs, one finger for the fastball, two fingers for the curve, and three fingers for the change of pace. The first inning was kind of long, but we got out of it all right. Paul didn't have too much. In the middle of the second; he called me out to the mound. "Mike," he said, "call for that two-finger ball more. I can get more on it." Then I realized that Paul had been gripping the ball with the number of fingers I put down. On the one-finger grip, which called for a fastball, he had been throwing a one-finger pitch.

Mike Ryba
catcher (1935–38),
on Paul Dean

The new owners made an announcement: No beer waiters, peanut venders, or score card boys will annoy patrons during games. Boys may sell score cards only before games. None after.

Frank DeHaas Robison and Mathew Stanley Robison

The American Baseball and Exhibition Co. (circa 1899–1910)

To amuse himself and onlookers, Pepper Martin would bounce a ball off the end of a bat while walking all the way from center field to the dugout. Still bouncing the ball on the bat with one arm, he would tip his hat to the fans in the first row and disappear down the dugout steps.

Doug Feldmann

If Sam Breadon would fall in a mud puddle, he would come out with a gold watch in his hand.

Enos Slaughter

on the longtime Cardinals owner

I got my signing bonus—a ham sandwich and a glass of milk—and was sent back home to get ready to leave for the minor leagues the next day.

Red Schoendienst

The good thing about him was he didn't snore.

Stan Musial

on longtime road roommate
Red Schoendienst

Any ballplayer that don't sign autographs for little kids isn't an American. He's a communist.

Rogers Hornsby

Slim Sallee was a blithe spirit who demonstrated the quirkiness that seems to come with being a big-league southpaw. He was an Ohio farmboy who was made nostalgic by the sight of horse-drawn milk wagons, and frequently he was up at sunrise riding the wagons and helping the drivers in their house deliveries.

Donald Honig

Sallee pitched for St. Louis from 1908 to 1916.

Run everything out, and be in by twelve.

Red Schoendienst

on what he expected from his players in 1968

A full mind is an empty bat.

Branch Rickey

He wore his hair so long at one time that it caught fire during a backyard cookout in St. Louis.

Bill Borst

on catcher Ted Simmons

On one particularly blazing-hot summer afternoon, Steve sought the only shade available, cast by the edge of the right-field grandstand. Somewhere he found a Japanese paper parasol and, holding it over his head, trotted out to his position the next inning. When the umpire refused to allow the game to proceed, with the right fielder standing under an umbrella, Evans reluctantly folded it up and threw it away, yelling at the umpire, "How would you like to stand out in the sun without an umbrella?" To which the perspiring ump yelled back, "Dammit, I *am* standing out in this sun without an umbrella!"

Donald Honig
*on outfielder Steve Evans
(1909–13) in 1911*

"Young man, I'd rather trade places with you than with any man in the country," to which Pepper replied, "Fine, Judge, if we can swap salaries too."

Donald Honig
on an exchange between baseball Commissioner Landis, making $60,000 to Martin's $4,500, after the 1931 World Series, in which Martin starred

A banner brought to Busch Memorial Stadium, on July 12, 1975, read: "We Hlove Hrabosky Hbanner Hday."

Robert L. Tiemann
author

He had the ability of taking a bad situation and making it immediately worse.

Branch Rickey
on Leo Durocher

Baseball has been very good to me since I quit trying to play it.

Whitey Herzog

Give me what I want and I'll take care of myself.

Marty Marion

to Branch Rickey during contract negotiations in 1941. Rickey, a notorious tightwad with Cardinal money, had told Marion, "Accept my terms and I'll take care of you." Marion, a strong negotiator himself, reportedly was the only Cardinal in the early 1940s making more than Rickey's airtight salary ceiling of $12,500

Put 'er there, Henry. I'm sure glad to be here 'cause I've heard so much about you. But I'm sorry, pardner, I'm a-gonna have to make pussycats out of your Tigers.

Dizzy Dean

to automobile entrepreneur Henry Ford before the start of the 1934 World Series

Anybody with ability can play in the big leagues. But to be able to trick people year in and year out the way I did, I think that was a much greater feat.

Bob Uecker

catcher (1964–65)/well-known broadcaster

Two stars and a bum.

Tony La Russa

on the fact that there have been only three shortstops to start a game in the major leagues at the age of 18: Alex Rodriguez, Robin Yount, and Tony La Russa

The way to catch a knuckleball is to wait until it stops rolling and then pick it up.

Bob Uecker

Bob Gibson is the luckiest pitcher I've ever seen. He always pitches on the day the other team doesn't score any runs.

Tim McCarver

catcher (1959–61, 1963–69, 1973–74)

The only thing you know about pitching is that you can't hit it.

Bob Gibson

to Tim McCarver

Bob Gibson pitches as though he's double-parked.

Vin Scully

longtime Los Angeles Dodgers broadcaster

The difference between playing at home and on the road is that on the road you can't go down to the kitchen to get a cup of coffee in the morning in your underwear.

Andy Van Slyke

outfielder (1983–86)

One time we were playing Houston. Al Hrabosky went behind the mound and threw the ball into his glove, the way he did, like he was mad. And he missed the glove! I think the next three or four guys hit ropes off him, because he lost his concentration.

Bob Forsch

If he feels that bad about striking out, imagine what he feels like at a funeral.

Bob Forsch

to manager Whitey Herzog,
on teammate Willie McGee,
sulking after a rare strikeout

Cut-up Bob Uecker practiced catching fly balls in batting practice before Game 1 of the 1964 World Series with a borrowed tuba.

Bruce Chadwick

author

CARDINAL LEGENDS

BRANCH RICKEY, ONE OF the best judges of talent in the game's history, believed that Chick Hafey—if blessed with normal eyesight and good health—might have become the best right-handed hitter baseball had ever known.

Rob Rains

on the Hall of Fame left fielder who played from 1924 through 1931

The immortal Cy Young headed the pitching staff [1899–1900]; he had won 30 or more victories in three seasons for Cleveland and was to close his memorable major-league career twelve years later with the majestic total of 511 victories.

Frederick G. Lieb

Young won 26 games for the Cardinals in 1899, leading the National League in complete games (40). The following year he won 19, with a league-leading four shutouts. His Cardinal years came right in the middle of his 22-year major-league career.

I'd rather him pitch a crucial game for me drunk, than anyone I've ever known sober. He was that good.

Rogers Hornsby
on Grover Cleveland Alexander

National League star Grover Cleveland Alexander got there with a pitch that took considerably longer to reach the plate; but when it did arrive, the pitch was exactly where he wanted it to be— and the last place the batter expected it to be.

Jim Murray

Los Angeles Times
columnist

Don't get the idea that Rogers Hornsby was merely a slap hitter who just put the bat on the ball. He was one of the most feared power hitters of his day. Twice he led the league in homers, with 42 in 1922 and 39 in 1925. Four times he led the league in RBIs, with a high of 152 in 1922.

Tim McCarver

Rogers Hornsby

Never go to a movie picture show. It's bad for your eyes.

Rogers Hornsby

The Rajah's advice to young hitters

In 1924, Jesse Haines pitched the first no-hitter in Cardinals history, shutting down the Boston Braves, 5–0, at Sportsman's Park. Haines spent 18 years with the Cardinals, the longest pitching tenure in club history, and he won 210 games, second on the Cards' all-time list to Bob Gibson's 251.

Rob Rains

Haines pitched for St. Louis from 1920 to 1937.

Frankie Frisch was the best money player I ever saw. If he had been on a tail-end ball club, he couldn't have done as well. It had to mean something. He could throw, he could field, he was smart, and he knew how to play the hitters. He was just a baseball player. He couldn't stand to lose. Frisch couldn't stand mistakes, because he was so perfect himself. He could do everything, and he thought everyone else could do it the same way.

Spud Davis

Competitive fire made him an odd mixture of fun and fury in his career.

Bob Broeg
on Frankie Frisch

Dizzy Dean is just a kid and this is only his second season. He has the chance to be rated with the Christy Mathewsons, the Walter Johnsons, and the Grover Cleveland Alexanders. This Cardinal star has everything a great pitcher needs— more smoke than a burning oil well, a fine curve ball, good control, a cool head, and plenty of heart.

Grantland Rice

legendary sportswriter, 1933

As a ballplayer, Dizzy Dean was a natural phenomenon, like the Grand Canyon or the Great Barrier Reef. Nobody ever taught him baseball, and he never had to learn.

Red Smith

sports columnist, New York Herald Tribune

When the Cardinals booked a rodeo as a pre-game feature to help draw people to the closing game of the schedule, Dizzy joined in. He missed lassoing a calf from the back of his horse, so he jumped down and wrestled the calf to the ground as the crowd cheered.

Jack Kavanagh

Despite a nickname that suggested he was a little flaky, when Dizzy Dean stood on that mound, there was nothing at all funny about him. If anything, he stood on that mound as a tall picture of fury. Few had his competitiveness or his meanness.

Peter Golenbock

Dizzy Dean

Anybody who's ever had the privilege of seein' me play ball knows that I am the greatest pitcher in the world.

Dizzy Dean

It ain't braggin' if you go out and do it.

Dizzy Dean

If Satch and I were pitching on the same team, we'd cinch the pennant by July 4 and go fishing until World Series time.

Dizzy Dean
on Satchel Paige

Of 123,000,000 people in this country, 99 percent are more interested in Dizzy Dean than the president of the United States.

Arthur Brisbane
editor/author/columnist

I beat Carl Hubbell four times in 1934. Diz didn't beat him once, but nobody talks about that.

Paul Dean

Several of the game's greatest hitters from the era said that his fastball was, without question, the most powerful in baseball.

Doug Feldmann
on Dizzy Dean

That ball came up there so fast it jumped like a jackrabbit when it crossed the plate.

Al Lopez
19-year major-league catcher
(1928, 1930–47),
on facing Dizzy Dean

I guess there never will be another like me.

Dizzy Dean

There's nobody like him, and there ain't been in years. He's as great as Mathewson, Alexander, and Johnson were in their day.

Paul Dean
pitcher (1934–39),
on brother Dizzy

To date, Dizzy Dean has the fewest number of career wins (150) than any pitcher in the Hall of Fame. However, the impact he made during his peak (1932–37) was truly lasting. His talent was coupled with a love of the game that entertained spectators while simultaneously intimidating opponents.

Doug Feldmann

Dizzy Dean was an original, a character that Mark Twain or Ring Lardner might have conjured. Sprung from a background of rural poverty and hardship, Dean was perceived as a prime slice of American hayseed but never lost his sense of humor, his gusto approach to life, nor his ability to charm those around him. He was a refreshing gale of optimism in those bleak, flat, and sour Depression years.

Donald Honig

The twin poisons of sport.

Grantland Rice
on the Dean brothers

Along with possessing one of the game's keenest minds, Leo Durocher was loud of voice, sharp of tongue, and provocative. Few men in the game's history ever had as many devoted admirers or as many sworn enemies as the man who came to be known as "the Lip."

Donald Honig

He was one of the most talented players ever to play for the Cardinals. In 17 years in the major leagues, Medwick batted .324, claimed the RBI title three consecutive years, and in 1937 won the Triple Crown and was named Most Valuable Player. During his era, only John Mize and Mel Ott outslugged him.

Tex Carleton
pitcher (1932–34),
on Joe Medwick

While in the minor leagues, he was dubbed "the Duck" by a female fan who likened his gait to that of a mallard. A local newspaperman made the name stick, and Joe Medwick was ornery with the media ever since.

Doug Feldmann

I have two good friends in this world: buckerinoes [money] and base hits. If I get base hits, I will get buckerinoes.

Joe "Ducky" Medwick

He won the Triple Crown in 1937 and remains the last National Leaguer to accomplish that feat.

Rob Rains

on Ducky Medwick

Branch Rickey was an interesting guy, a man of many paradoxes. He had a very healthy interest in world affairs. He read widely. He was a devout member of the Methodist Church, a deacon. He probably was a virgin when he married his wife. You know how he didn't go to ball games on Sunday. He did not like to discuss it, not with newspaper people or anybody else, except to say that as a kid when he left home to go play baseball, he promised his mother he would not go to a ballpark on Sunday. Of course, he was criticized for that many times by sportswriters who thought it was hypocritical because he shared in the profits of the Sunday doubleheaders, all right.

Gene Karst

He would be remembered bitterly by his players for his low salaries. For several generations of Cardinal and, later, Brooklyn Dodger players, the name of Branch Rickey would be spoken as though uttering a curse.

Peter Golenbock

Though his playing and managerial records were not impressive, he became the architect of the Cardinals' winning ways. Rickey was an astute judge of talent and a shrewd executive. Founder of the farm system, his skill in scouting and developing players was instrumental in the Cardinals' enormous success from 1926 through 1946, a period during which the Cards won nine pennants and six World Series.

Rob Rains

on the front-office genius of Branch Rickey

Johnny Mize was, without a doubt, one of the best curveball hitters I've ever seen. A pitcher could throw him his best breaking ball and the Big Cat would rip it right out of the ballpark. What a great swing he had! It gave him the rare ability to be both a great power hitter and a good contact hitter. That combination also resulted in the highest slugging average in the National League during the first three years I was up.

Enos Slaughter

His 43 home runs in 1940 led the majors and stood as the Cardinals' single-season record until the mark was broken by Mark McGwire in 1998.

Rob Rains

on Cardinals slugger Johnny Mize (1936–41)

National Baseball Hall of Fame Library, Cooperstown, N.Y.

Enos "Country" Slaughter

Johnny Mize was a great, great hitter. In my book, you have to put him up there with the great hitters of all time, not only as a power hitter but as a contact hitter as well. The amazing thing about him is that he was a tough guy to strike out.

Ralph Kiner
Hall of Famer and seven-time consecutive National League home run champion with the Pittsburgh Pirates (1946–52)

Enos Slaughter is one of the greatest kids to come into the league in years.

Frankie Frisch

Playing right field, rookie Enos Slaughter would soon become his era's symbol of fervent, nonstop hustle. If there was a prototype Cardinal, it was Slaughter. He was tough, daring, and absolutely dedicated to making that 360-foot trip around the bases as quickly as possible. He could run, he possessed a strong arm; he was a Carolina country boy, and he was a hungry player, willing to take chances. No player ever brought more devotion to the game or to his employers.

Donald Honig

Red covered a lot of ground and could go back on fly balls to center and right field better than most people I've ever seen. He was a very steady player. He had the greatest hands I've ever seen, and he was as good a fundamental player as you ever wanted to see. He almost never made a mistake.

Stan Musial

on Red Schoendienst

One thing I never realized is that the Redhead is as good hitting right-handed as he is left-handed. He's the same as he is from the left side—a good line-drive hitter.

Johnny Keane

on the switch-hitting Schoendienst, still fifth all-time in Cardinals hits

Red Schoendienst

Curt Flood could go deep in the count, hit behind the runner, and steal a base. Don Drysdale called him the toughest out in the National League.

Tim McCarver

Only one player in the history of baseball has ever matched pioneer Jackie Robinson in the intensity of his competitive spirit. That player was Bob Gibson, the premier pitcher in the history of St. Louis baseball.

Bill Borst

Bob Gibson was among the most competitive people I've ever been around. He never said anything to anybody. He just went out and played.

Red Schoendienst

Bob Gibson was a pitcher that pitched under great physical handicap. He loved to win but had that bad knee. He never felt 100 percent. I always admired his courage.

Butch Yatkeman

longtime Cardinals clubhouse manager

If Bob Gibson was the intestines of the Cardinals, Musial the heart, Marion the spirit, and Rickey the mind, Lou Brock should always be known as the bloodstream.

Bill Borst

A good leadoff man sets the tone of the game. He sets the table, as I call it, and also can arrange the way the other players sit at the table. He jump-starts things, is an igniter. You usually can't rattle a leadoff guy.

Lou Brock

Bob Gibson

To most people, the distance between first base and second base is 90 feet. To Lou Brock, it was 13 steps.

Rob Rains

Lou was the most arrogant player I ever saw, just as Maury Wills had been when he was in his prime. He was going to take that lead, he was going to steal the base, and there wasn't anything anyone could do about it. A pitcher could step off, could throw over, he wasn't going to stop Brock from stealing.

Jack Buck

When Steve [Carlton] and I die, we are going to be buried in the same cemetery, sixty feet, six inches apart.

Tim McCarver

Ozzie Smith

His coverage at shortstop threatened to wear out the word "spectacular." He had reflexes of feline quickness, a strong arm, and moves in the face of sliding runners that were nothing less than acrobatic.

Donald Honig
on Ozzie Smith

When he went up for his last at-bat, I looked up at the scoreboard and saw his stats: 69 home runs, 144 RBIs, and I'm thinking, "Look at that; that's not a season, that's a career."

Tom Lampkin
catcher (1997–98),
on best friend and teammate
Mark McGwire, in 1998

McGwire hit home run No. 70 in that last at-bat, closing with 147 RBIs.

SHRINE TO NO. 6

OF ALL THE TEAMS I've seen so far, Musial is the best.

Eddie Sawyer
*manager, Philadelphia Phillies
(1948–52, 1958–60),
when asked to assess the
National League in 1948*

I believe the joy of getting paid as a man to play a boy's game kept me going longer than many other players. Whether I was getting $100 a month in Class D or $100,000 a season in the majors, I never lost the feeling that I had the best way in the country to make a living, meager or plentiful.

Stan Musial

That kid was born to play baseball.

Billy Southworth
*manager (1929, 1940–45),
after watching the rookie Musial
play 12 games at the end of the
1941 season, during which he
hit .426*

He stood in a peculiar, corkscrew-like stance, "like a kid peeking around the corner to see if the cops are coming," said one pitcher.

John Devaney
author

His nickname, "Stan the Man," had come by way of Brooklyn, where fans moaned every time they saw "that man" coming to the plate.

Rob Rains

Pressure? I don't think anyone ever explained to him what it meant. We were fighting for our lives and this kid comes up cool as ice and starts hitting line drives that made the ball bleed.

Ernie White
pitcher (1940–43),
on Musial's first call-up to the
Cardinals, at the tail-end of the
1941 season

Musial was the Cardinals' fourth true superstar. Hornsby had offended people with his blunt candor, Medwick with his surliness, and even the lovable Dean had found detractors with his bragging and his bursts of temperament. The ever friendly Musial, however, was perfect.

Donald Honig

Baseball's perfect warrior, baseball's perfect knight.

Ford Frick

former commissioner of baseball, on Musial

Stan comes sauntering up to the plate and asks me how my family's making out. Before I can answer him, he's on third base.

Joe Garagiola

on onetime teammate Musial

The 1948 season saw Stan Musial at his absolute peak. In winning his third MVP Award, the 27-year-old star won his third batting crown with a career high .376 average, as well as leading in hits (230), doubles (46), triples (18), runs (135), RBIs (131), total bases (429), and slugging (.702).

Donald Honig

I do not consciously feel any thrill out of a good play or a winning hit.

Stan Musial

While Brooklyn jubilated in its "Boys of Summer," St. Louis has its own "Man for All Seasons."

Bill Borst

Hit it on the dry side.

Stan Musial

on how to handle a spitball

National Baseball Hall of Fame Library, Cooperstown, N.Y.

Stan "the Man" Musial

You could make a study of Musial's life and learn how to be a decent human being. He did not have a shred of ego or temperament. He was always serene, no matter the situation. How he was able to maintain this serenity, this calm, and be at all times the most self-confident, highly concentrated, and zealous competitor that he also was, is surely worth reflecting upon.

Branch Rickey

As long as you see those red birds on a Cardinal uniform, you will hear people telling stories about Stan Musial and what he was like as a ballplayer and a human being. It would take a full page to list, in small type, all the records he holds or shares.

John Devaney

When he retired he had gone to bat more often than anyone except Ty Cobb, collected more doubles than anyone except Tris Speaker, hit for more total bases than anybody. He ranks with Ted Williams, Babe Ruth, and Cobb among the four greatest left-handed hitters of all time.

John Devaney

In 1959 Musial was not hitting well, and some people at Sportsman's Park booed him. The next morning ads appeared in the St. Louis newspapers, paid for by prominent people, publicly apologizing to Stan for the boos.

John Devaney

Stan hit five home runs, and by the end of the second game, I was convinced I'd seen the greatest ballplayer who ever lived. He was magnificent. To my 11-year-old eyes, he was the embodiment of everything good. To see him hit one home run was almost more excitement than I could stand, but five home runs in one day! I was hoarse from cheering and my hands were sore from clapping, but I knew I had witnessed history. A hero who meets the expectations of a little boy is very rare, but on that day in 1954, Stan "the Man" Musial met and surpassed my expectations. It was magic.

Jim Shucart

fan,
on Musial's performance for the
ages against the New York
Giants, May 2, 1954

I just throw him my best stuff, then run over to back up third.

Carl Erskine
Brooklyn Dodgers pitcher,
on Musial, 1948

Walk him. Pick him off of first base.

Joe Garagiola
catcher (1946–51),
on how to pitch to Stan Musial

In his career, Stan Musial hit nine grand slams . . . and added seven almost-grand slams, hitting seven bases-loaded triples.

Rob Rains

At nearly 43, Stan Musial bowed out briskly in 1963, not the Musial of old, but most certainly not an old Musial either.

Bob Broeg

Who would ever think that a guy could make so much money with a little piece of wood.

Gary Kolb

outfielder (1960, 1962–63), pondering Stan Musial's bat before The Man's last game as a Cardinal in 1963

When my son's friend is my teammate, I figure it's time to retire.

Stan Musial

when asked, on turning 43, why he wasn't going to play one more year. His reference was to fellow Cardinal Mike Shannon, who played high school baseball with Stan's son

If I didn't quit, the Cardinals never would have won in 1964.

Stan Musial

referencing the trade in 1964 that brought young left fielder Lou Brock to St. Louis following Musial's 1963 retirement

Stan jumped out of the dugout, walked to the batting cage, and watched me swing. Then he took me over to the side and he talked hitting to me for 15 minutes. Me, a nothing. I will never forget his kindness. When he finished, he slapped me on the back and told me to keep swinging.

Chuck Connors

actor (The Rifleman)/outfielder Chicago Cubs, Brooklyn Dodgers, on the occasion when the struggling young Cubs outfielder asked Musial for a few batting tips

It's ridiculous that we are gathered here tonight to honor a man who made more than 7,000 outs.

Bob Prince

longtime Pittsburgh Pirates broadcaster, at Stan Musial's retirement dinner

MAJOR
MOMENTS

I RECKON I'D BETTER strike him out.

Grover Cleveland Alexander
pitcher (1926–29),
to manager/second baseman Rogers
Hornsby, on entering Game 7 of the
1926 World Series in relief against the
Yankees, with the bases loaded and
two out in the seventh inning, facing
Tony Lazzeri. Alexander, who had
pitched a complete Game 6 victory
the day before, then reportedly par-
tied long into the night, struck out
Lazzeri, and the Cardinals held on
to win their first World Series crown

"Sunny Jim" Bottomley

National Baseball Hall of Fame Library, Cooperstown, N.Y.

The date was Sept. 16, 1924. For Jim Bottomley, it was an afternoon of delectable mayhem at Brooklyn's Ebbets Field that is still in the record books. The final score was St. Louis 17 and Brooklyn 3, with 12 of the Cardinal runs being driven in by Sunny Jim (still the single greatest one-game RBI performance in major-league history, though tied by another Cardinal, Mark Whiten, in 1993). Bottomley did it this way: two-run single in the first inning; one-run double in the second inning; grand-slam home run in the fourth; two-run homer in the sixth; two-run single in the seventh; one-run single in the ninth.

Donald Honig

1924 was the year, under those hot Missouri skies of long ago, that Rogers Hornsby scaled the Mount Everest of twentieth-century batting averages with a mark of .424, a figure of such regal superiority that no one has since come close to approaching it. He achieved it by coming to the plate 536 times and collecting 227 hits.

Donald Honig

Alex had had a few drinks the night before, but he wasn't drunk, because Rog [manager Rogers Hornsby] had told him he might need Alex the next day. Alex wasn't sleeping in the pen and he wasn't hung over—he stood there and told us exactly how he was going to pitch Lazzeri, and his mind was sharp as a tack.

Les Bell

third baseman (1923–27),
on the oft-told story of the physi-
cal condition of pitcher Grover
Cleveland Alexander upon enter-
ing Game 7 of the 1926 World
Series in the seventh inning, just
before recording one of the most
famous strikeouts in history, with
New York Yankees rookie Tony
Lazzeri at the plate and the
bases full. Alexander was sum-
moned to protect the Cardinals'
narrow 3–2 lead

The four-pitch strikeout of Tony Lazzeri, commemorated on Grover Cleveland Alexander's Hall of Fame plaque, represents just about the most tense moment in the history of the World Series. The 3–2 lead held up for the championship when Ruth, walking on a questionable borderline pitch with two out in the ninth, was thrown out trying a surprise steal, O'Farrell to Hornsby.

Bob Broeg

on the pressure-packed ending of the 1926 World Series, won by St. Louis over the New York Yankees

For Rogers Hornsby, tagging the Babe ranked as the greatest moment of his career.

Bob Broeg

on the ending to the 1926 World Series

That's the one they call the Pepper Martin World Series. Pepper went hog wild, got 12 hits and stole a passel of bases. [A's catcher] Mickey Cochrane never had a chance. Every time poor Mickey looked up, there was Pepper sliding around to one base or another.

Burleigh Grimes
pitcher (1930–31, 1933–34)

Great people seem to rise to great occasions, and Dizzy Dean did so on Sept. 30, 1934. He was going after his 30th win, something which no one had done in the National League since 1917, and which no one has done in the Senior Circuit since.

Doug Feldmann

In 1933 Dizzy Dean had his first 20-game winning season. Before the month of July was over, he had made headlines with his record-breaking 17-strikeout game in Chicago.

Jack Kavanagh

How would you feel? You get three itsy-bitsy hits off the big brother in the first game, and then you look around and there's the little brother with biscuits from the same table to throw at you.

Casey Stengel
Brooklyn Dodgers manager (1934–36),
on the Sept. 21, 1934, double-header loss to the Dean brothers.
Paul Dean's nightcap no-hitter was just the second hitless gem in Cardinals history

The baseball equivalent to a shooting star, Dizzy Dean's career virtually ended—for all intents and purposes—at the 1937 All-Star Game in Washington, D.C. Following a home run off the bat of Lou Gehrig, the Cleveland Indians' Earl Averill lined a ball off Dean's left foot and broke the big toe. Trying to pitch the Cardinals to another pennant, he attempted to come back from the injury later in the summer despite still having discomfort in the toe. The pain that remained caused him to alter his delivery, and the result was an unnatural arm motion. His changed style put extreme stress on his elbow, and he had a sore arm for the rest of the year.

Doug Feldmann

The last game was tied 2–2 in the ninth inning, with Walker Cooper on first base, when Whitey Kurowski hit a home run off Red Ruffing to win it.

Stan Musial

on the Cardinals' Game 5 victory over the Yankees in the 1942 World Series. After dropping the first game to New York, St. Louis won four straight

Playing despite the death of their father earlier in the day, the Coopers, Mort and Walker, formed the Cards' battery in Game 2 of the 1943 World Series. Mort won, 4–3.

Rob Rains

It was the quietest World Series ever.

Luke Sewell

manager, St. Louis Browns
(1941–46),
on the 1944 "Streetcar Series"
between the city of St. Louis's
American League and National
League champions, won by the
Cardinals four games to two

This was the first World Series played entirely west of the Mississippi. St. Louis became only the third city ever to have the Series entirely to itself. The other one-city Series took place in Chicago in 1906; New York in 1921, 1922, 1923, 1936, 1937; and Brooklyn and the Yankees in 1941. It was dubbed the "Streetcar Series" and was played without any days off for travel, since both teams played in the same park.

Bill Borst

on the St. Louis intra-city World
Series in 1944

The famous "Trolley Series" has also been dubbed the "Strikeout Series" because of the record number of strike-outs in a six-game Series—49 by Cardinal pitchers and 43 by Brownie hurlers. In the final two games, all eight Brownie pinch hitters struck out.

**James V. Young and
Arthur F. McClure**

authors

The Series' Most Valuable Player, Marty Marion, hit only .227 and had just a pair of runs batted in, yet his defense was awe-inspiring. The ubiquitous shortstop was the standout competitor on the field in each of the six games. He had 22 assists and seven putouts without making an error.

Bill Borst

*on the 1944 World Series and
National League regular-season
MVP*

After Harry Walker hit that ball, my eyes were riveted on the baseline and my mind was totally focused on making it to home plate as fast as my legs would carry me. By the time Johnny Pesky realized I was going for the plate, he didn't have a chance. I kicked up some dust and a few pebbles, as I slid into the plate. But with the throw drawing catcher Roy Partee out four or five steps in front of home, I could have made it just as well standing up.

Enos Slaughter

on his legendary eighth-inning "Mad Dash for Home" that proved the decisive run in the Cardinals' 4–3 Game 7 win in the 1946 World Series

The most memorable event of my first season in St. Louis came on a Sunday afternoon, May 2, 1954, in a rain-delayed doubleheader against the Giants. Stan Musial hit five home runs, three in the first game, two in the second, and might have had another with the longest ball he hit all day, but it was to straightaway center and was caught by Willie Mays.

Jack Buck

Maybe I'll end this right here.

Stan Musial

to Yogi Berra, American League All-Star catcher,
in the bottom of the 12th inning of the 1955 All-Star Game at County Stadium in Milwaukee. Moments later Musial sent a first-pitch fastball out of the park for a walk-off home run and a 6–5 National League victory

The turning point in the 1964 World Series came in the sixth inning of Game 4. The Yankees, leading the Series two games to one, were ahead 3–0. Another win and New York would hold a commanding lead. After the Cardinals loaded the bases against Al Downing, team captain Ken Boyer pulled St. Louis ahead by hammering a pitch into the left-field seats. Boyer, the National League's MVP that season, later called the grand slam the highlight of his career.

Rob Rains

The [1967 World Series] was a coming-out party for Lou Brock and Bob Gibson, who played great as we edged the Red Sox in seven games. Brock hit .414 and stole a record seven bases, and Gibson won three games, including Game 7.

Red Schoendienst

In 1967 Bob Gibson, fully recovered from the broken leg he suffered from a ball batted by Roberto Clemente, was back on the mound for the Cardinals. Gibson's pitching, combined with Lou Brock's larceny on the bases, catapulted the Cards to another championship. Brock was the "Wild Card" who played the bases as if they belonged to him. He pilfered seven bases for a new World Series record. He also chipped in with a tape-measure homer in the sixth game.

Bill Borst

A final-day crowd of 35,188 saw Gibson fan 10 men and allow just three hits and two runs. For the Series, Gibson fanned 26 men in three complete-game wins, allowing just three earned runs. He was voted Series MVP, but a couple others deserved accolades. Brock hit .414, scored eight runs, and stole seven bases, while Maris hit .385 and led the team with seven RBIs.

Mel Freese

*on the 1967 World Series,
taken by St. Louis, four games
to three, over the Boston Red Sox
for the Cardinals' eighth world
championship crown*

Gibson in 1968 created a landmark season, a season of such impressive dimensions that it remains like fire in the baseball skies.

Donald Honig

Gibson chalked up a 22–9 won-lost record, but his stellar 1.12 ERA (for pitchers throwing 300 or more innings) is a standard for the ages. That figure, according to Honig, is to the pitching fraternity what Ted Williams's .406 batting average in 1941 is to hitters.

On Oct. 2, 1968, as Tiger after Tiger came to the plate, Gibby mowed them down with an ease and perfection rivaled by no other pitcher in the history of the fall classic. He fanned 17 batters to set a new single-game mark, erasing Sandy Koufax's 15.

Bill Borst

Get back there, dammit!

Bob Gibson

to catcher Tim McCarver, who had headed out to the mound to inform Gibson he had just tied Sandy Koufax's World Series single-game strikeout mark of 15, in the ninth inning during Game 1 of the 1968 World Series against Detroit. Gibson went on to record two more K's to establish a new Series record of 17

In 1969, on September 15 at Busch Stadium, Steve Carlton set a new one-game major-league record by nailing 19 New York Mets on strikes. Unfortunately, he also fed a couple of two-run homers to Ron Swoboda, enough for a 4–3 Mets victory.

Donald Honig

On Oct. 7, 1969, the Cardinals sent Curt Flood, Tim McCarver, Joe Hoerner, and outfielder Byron Browne to the Phillies in exchange for Richie Allen, Cookie Rojas, and Jerry Johnson. The idea of being traded offended Flood. He sued to become a free agent, asserting that the "reserve clause" was unconstitutional. The Supreme Court, however, upheld the status quo. Flood never reported to Philadelphia, choosing to sit out the 1970 season.

Donald Honig

I never expected to get one, because I'm a high-ball pitcher and high-ball pitchers don't pitch no-hitters.

Bob Gibson

after logging his one and only career no-hitter, Aug. 14, 1971, against Pittsburgh

For Joe Torre, 1971 was a spectacular season. Playing third base, he won the batting title with a .363 average, led in hits with 230, and RBIs with 137, hit 24 home runs, and became the 11th Cardinal to win the MVP Award.

Donald Honig

With Reggie Smith using a stopwatch as always, figuring pitch-to-catch-to-second base at 3.5 seconds, about a split-second slower than Brock made it with his 13 strides to baseball immortality, No. 20 slid in easily ahead of Bob Boone's throw to shortstop Larry Bowa: 105!

Bob Broeg

on Lou Brock's record-setting 105th stolen base of the season, Sept. 10, 1974, against Philadelphia, breaking Maury Wills's 12-year-old mark

It was not necessarily Lou Brock's stealing a base, but one of those events in history where a person's performance on the field surpasses a record that has been set by a tremendous ball player. Just to be a part of that has been fulfilling to me.

Lou Brock

after breaking Ty Cobb's 50-year-old record with his 893rd career stolen base, on Aug. 29, 1977, against the San Diego Padres

The 2–2 pitch, a breaking ball. Hit off the pitcher! To the third baseman! No play! Base hit 3,000 for Lou Brock! Pan-de-monium! Brock is mobbed at first—a bullet back to the mound. Brock strode across the base and into the history books.

Jack Buck

calling the play-by-play as Brock recorded his 3,000th career base hit, Aug. 13, 1979, against the Chicago Cubs' Dennis Lamp at Busch Stadium

I guess I'd better send my fingers to Cooperstown.

Dennis Lamp

Chicago Cubs pitcher, who gave up Lou Brock's 3,000th career base hit. The smash back up the middle glanced off Lamp's pitching hand

A guy told me he was listening on the radio and drove off the highway. Another guy told me he was barbecuing and knocked his grill over. I guess it shocked them.

Glenn Brummer

catcher (1981–84), on his startling game-winning steal of home with two out in the 12th inning against the Giants, Aug. 22, 1982. At the time, St. Louis was in first place with a one-game edge over Philadelphia

On October 15 at Milwaukee, Willie McGee robbed Paul Molitor and Gorman Thomas of extra base hits with great catches in the first and ninth innings. In between, he hit two home runs and drove in four runs to pace a 6–2 victory.

Mel Freese

on Game 3 of the 1982 World Series vs. the Brewers

Getting spectacular all-around play from Willie McGee, key hitting from catcher Darrell Porter and first baseman Keith Hernandez, and standout pitching, St. Louis forced a seventh game in the 1982 World Series against Milwaukee. The Cards won the finale, 6–3. Bruce Sutter provided St. Louis with one of its greatest baseball moments when he struck out the Brewers' Gorman Thomas to end the Series.

Rob Rains

Go crazy, folks, go crazy! It's a home run, and the Cardinals have won the game by the score of 3 to 2 on a home run by The Wizard. . . . Go crazy!

Jack Buck

*St. Louis Cardinals broadcaster
(1954–59, 1961–2001),
on Ozzie Smith's walk-off home
run against Los Angeles to end
Game 5 of the 1985 NLCS*

To stay in the park, that ball would have had to hit the Goodyear blimp and come straight down.

Tom Niedenfuer

*Los Angeles Dodgers pitcher
(1981–87),
who served up the 1985 NLCS-
winning three-run home run to
Cardinals slugger Jack Clark in
the ninth inning of Game 6 at
Chavez Ravine*

Who 'n hell does he think he is, Babe Ruth?

Bob Broeg

after Ozzie Smith's Game 5-ending homer in the 1985 NLCS

I've been around the game 16 years; I've seen some guys do some unbelievable things, but nothing like tonight.

Ozzie Smith

on Mark Whiten's record-tying performance against the Cincinnati Reds, Sept. 7, 1993, at Riverfront Stadium, in which the Cardinals' center fielder drove in 12 runs and smacked four homers in a 15–2 St. Louis victory. His RBI output tied the 69-year-old major-league record set by Cardinals Hall of Famer Jim Bottomley back in 1924. The switch-hitting Whiten clubbed all four round-trippers left-handed

One cannot appreciate Mark McGwire's 70 home runs without the context of Babe Ruth and Roger Maris. Indeed, they were as much a part of the historic 1998 season as Mac and Sammy Sosa.

Tina Wright
author

McGwire's quick and majestic swing caught the pitch and sent it screaming toward the Stadium Club just below the upper deck in left field. It startled the well-dressed diners inside the Club, as it ricocheted off the protective glass in front of them. McGwire threw both hands up as he ran down the first-base line. In right field, Sosa smiled and applauded, patting his glove.

**George Castle and
Jim Rygelski**

authors,
on Mark McGwire's record-tying
61st home run in 1998

Preparing himself with the intense watch of the pitcher and slow back-and-forth waving of the bat, he was the only one oblivious to the popping of pocket-camera flashcubes all over the stadium, another ritual that had accompanied his every swing in a night game as he neared the record. Steve Trachsel's first pitch was knee high and over the plate. McGwire attacked it and sent a laser shot headed for the left-field corner. Fox broadcaster Tim McCarver would later say he thought it had enough force to go through the wall if not over it. It would be McGwire's shortest homer of the season, a computer measurement of 341 feet, but it would have the longest impact.

**George Castle and
Jim Rygelski**

*on McGwire's record-breaking
62nd home run in 1998*

It was a sweet, sweet run around the bases.

Mark McGwire

after homer No. 62

It's hard to fathom. Seventy's a really big number. I was in awe of myself, and I'm still in awe thinking about it.

Mark McGwire

on his record-setting accomplishment in 1998

Two grand slams in one inning? Sounds like something Mark McGwire would do. Well, he certainly was there—watching Fernando Tatis make history.

The Associated Press

on Tatis's monumental achieve-ment against the Los Angeles Dodgers, April 23, 1999, at Dodger Stadium. Tatis's eight RBIs in the third inning bettered the previous major-league mark of six in a single inning, as the Cardinals downed L.A., 12–5

It's probably the hardest I ever ran for a ball. It just faded into me.

Jim Edmonds

center fielder (2000–), preventing a big second inning in Game 7 of the 2004 NLCS against Houston, with a racing, headlong-diving, stomach-sliding catch in the left-center alley to rob the Astros' Brad Ausmus with two runners on. Clumps of grass kicked up as the seven-time Gold Glove winner hit the ground, sliding several feet

After Albert Pujols led off with a tiebreaking shot, the recently slumping Scott Rolen connected in a cold rain. The drives gave the Cardinals consecutive homers for the first time in their long, proud postseason history.

The Associated Press
Oct. 14, 2004,
on the back-to-back eighth-inning
shots that sent St. Louis past the
Houston Astros, 6–4, for a 2–0
lead in the National League
Championship Series

It's about damn time.

Cardinals teammates
to Scott Rolen,
after his two-homer performance
in the 2004 NLCS Game 2 triumph
over the Houston Astros snapped
the St. Louis third baseman's
postseason 0–for–14 hitting slump

Albert Pujols

Displaying the explosive firepower they used to win a major-league-best 105 games during the regular season, the Cardinals scored three runs in the sixth inning to erase a 2–1 deficit and defeated the Houston Astros, 5–2, in Game 7 of the 2004 National League Championship Series. Albert Pujols, named MVP of the NLCS, smacked an RBI double, and Scott Rolen smashed a two-run homer on consecutive pitches from seven-time Cy Young Award winner Roger Clemens, the rally sending the Astros home still without a World Series appearance in their 43-year history.

Chuck Johnson

USA TODAY

8

ST. LOUIS CARDINALS ALL-TIME TEAM

Lou Brock, Keith Hernandez, Red Schoendienst, Marty Marion, Mark McGwire, Willie McGee, Pepper Martin, Dizzy Dean, Ducky Medwick, Terry Moore, Frankie Frisch . . . and these are guys who didn't make the team!

It only points out the incredible depth of talent through the years that the St. Louis Cardinals have placed on the field. In future seasons, we likely may see the names Pujols, Rolen, and Edmonds among this elite nine. But tenure, that old benchmark of durability and consistency, merits a lot of weight against the prodigious marks being put up by today's young players still years away from their collective apex. So let the jawing begin. For your scrutinous review and argumentative pleasure: the St. Louis Cardinals All-Time Team.

"Sunny Jim" Bottomley played for the Cardinals in the twenties and thirties and led the National League in triples, home runs, and RBIs in 1928. It isn't often a guy leads the league in triples and home runs in the same year, a rare combination of power and speed.

Tim McCarver

"SUNNY JIM" BOTTOMLEY
First base (1922–32)

Some might say that beating out Hernandez and McGwire for the Cardinals' all-time team might be his greatest achievement, but the big first baseman left far more sub-stantive stuff on record during his 11-year career in St. Louis.

The Hall of Famer posted one timeless mark, a figure that still stands and that took 69 years to tie—most RBIs in a game, 12. That hallowed standard, set at Ebbets Field in Brooklyn, on Sept. 16, 1924, was tied by a latter-day Cardinal, Mark Whiten, in 1993. Against the Dodgers that day, Bottomley singled three times, hit a double, and smashed two home runs.

Nine times in his 11 St. Louis seasons he hit .300 or better, logging 100 RBIs or more six times as a Cardinal. In his 1928 National League MVP year, Bottomley tagged 20 triples, 31 homers, and 136 RBIs. Of his 187 hits that year, half (93) were for extra bases.

In 1925, the skipper batted .403, hit 39 home runs, and drove in 143 runs to take his second Triple Crown. For Rogers Hornsby, it was now six batting and six slugging titles in a row—a dominance unprecedented and unequaled in league annals. Over the five-year period 1921–25, the Cardinals' clockwork hitter averaged .402.

Donald Honig

People ask me what I do in winter when there's no baseball. I'll tell you what I do. I stare out the window and wait for spring.

Rogers Hornsby

ROGERS HORNSBY
Second base (1915–26, 1933)

A two-time Triple Crown winner (1922, '25), Hornsby is considered the greatest right-handed hitter in the history of the game. Though often surly and cantankerous in personality, "frank to the point of being cruel and as subtle as a belch," as sports-writer Lee Allen once observed, "the Rajah" knew hitting, finishing behind only Ty Cobb in lifetime batting average (.358).

Perhaps his greatest achievement was maintaining a batting average above .400 for five consecutive years (1921–25), with his astronomical .424, recorded in 1924, the highest modern batting average ever posted. The six-time National League batting champion hit .300 or better in 13 full seasons.

As player-manager in 1926, Hornsby brought the Cardinals their first-ever world championship.

Ken Boyer, with a power bat, sure glove, and strong arm, was destined to become the greatest third baseman in Cardinal history.

Donald Honig

Beneath the good humor in Kenny, there was Gas House, and lots of it.

John Devaney

on Ken Boyer

KEN BOYER
Third base (1955–65)

The Cardinals' captain, a seven-time National League All-Star, combined melliflu-ous grace and consistency with underrated power. Though often thought of as a lesser fielder in comparison with younger brother Cletis, the New York Yankees' third base-man of the 1960s, the elder Boyer earned five Gold Glove awards with St. Louis.

Not unlike his fielding prowess, Boyer was seldom thought of as a power hitter yet logged enough round-trippers to still rank second all-time in Cardinals annals in home runs (255).

His career highlight came in Game 4 of the 1964 World Series against the Yankees, when he clouted a grand slam to give St. Louis a crucial 4–3 win to even the Series at two games apiece. In addition, he is the only Cardinal ever to hit for the cycle twice.

The backflips. The horizontal leaps. The unlikely home run. Those are the thoughts that first come to mind when you think of Ozzie Smith.

Rob Rains

Ozzie Smith is not only the greatest defensive shortstop to ever play the game, but he's also a first-rate human being, a leader in the best sense of the word.

Whitey Herzog

OZZIE SMITH
Shortstop (1982–96)

Good field-no hit just never fit the athletic Smith. Regarded by most experts as the finest fielding shortstop ever, The Wizard was hardly a lightweight hitter, averaging .282 in 15 seasons with St. Louis and collecting nearly 2,500 hits overall, including four years with San Diego before being traded to the Cardinals.

In Smith's first season with St. Louis, in 1982, the Redbirds captured their last World Series crown. Three years later, he enjoyed his biggest moment at the plate, launching a walk-off home run that clinched Game 5 of the 1985 NLCS against Los Angeles; he batted .435 in that six-game series.

In the field, the incomparable Smith garnered 13 consecutive Gold Glove awards and was selected to 15 All-Star Games.

There is no greater pleasure in the world than walking up to the plate with men on base and knowing that you are feared.

Ted Simmons

catcher (1968–80)

Ted Simmons would have received much more consideration [for the Hall of Fame]—as the best catcher in the National League in the 1970s—had Johnny Bench been a carpenter or an accountant or something other than a ballplayer.

Big Klu

NetShrine.com discussion group, July 18, 2002

TED SIMMONS
Catcher (1968–80)

The switch-hitting Simmons, a .298 hitter over 13 seasons in St. Louis, while not of Gold Glove caliber behind the plate, worked well with pitchers and was tough and intelligent.

A solid contact hitter, Simmons established no less than eight major-league career batting records for catchers, including most hits, most singles, and most doubles—credentials that should place him in Cooperstown. Ultimately, he logged 21 seasons in the majors, including five with Milwaukee and three with Atlanta.

His resounding potential enabled the Cardinals to unload incumbent backstop Tim McCarver in 1970. "Simba" was a six-time All-Star as a Cardinal and caught more games than any catcher in club history.

The greatest player I ever saw was my own longtime teammate Stan Musial. I think Ted Williams was probably the greatest hitter I've ever seen, but between Ted and Musial, I'd have to take Stan as an all-around player over Williams.

Enos "Country" Slaughter

Stan Musial could have hit .300 with a fountain pen.

Joe Garagiola

STAN MUSIAL
Left field (1941–44, 1946–63)

The most prolific hitter in Cardinals history, The Man—an icon of immeasurable proportions—easily gets the nod for "Mr. Cardinal."

Musial's illustrious career, all in St. Louis, spanned 22 seasons. During that time he was a seven-time National League batting champion, three-time MVP, and starred on the victorious world championship teams of 1942, '44, and '46. When he retired after the 1963 season, his career hits total of 3,630 was second only to Ty Cobb.

Another unique mark set by Musial was his 24 All-Star Game appearances, tying him for tops all-time with Willie Mays and Henry Aaron. Baseball's perfect warrior/perfect knight was the first Cardinal in club history to have his number retired, in 1963.

Curt Flood had established himself as one of the premier center fielders in the league, the equal of Willie Mays. He could go get them with Mays, though he lacked Mays's powerful arm. However, Flood was more accurate. Flood had developed into a .300 hitter and a top-notch lead-off man but didn't have Mays's power.

Mel Freese

Free agency and arbitration, which are the reasons salaries have escalated to such lofty levels, would have happened sooner or later, with or without Flood. But Curt made it happen sooner because he was a man of courage and great principle who took a stand when it needed to be taken. And he took that stand at great personal sacrifice.

Tim McCarver

CURT FLOOD
Center field (1958–69)

He will always be known as the player who bravely bucked the system that had strangled player movement since the advent of the game. While the remnants of Curt Flood's landmark lawsuit linger, many forget the brilliance of Flood, the baseball player.

Defensively, he was compared to all the great center fielders, and as a hitter, Flood notched a career batting average of .293 in his 12 seasons in St. Louis. No Cardinals center fielder has collected more hits than Flood, and his .987 fielding percentage also outranks Terry Moore—considered the finest defensive center fielder of the 1930s and '40s—Willie McGee, and Pepper Martin, though it is matched by current star Jim Edmonds.

Flood was a three-time National League All-Star selection and seven-time Gold Glove winner.

The fiercely competitive Slaughter was a mainstay in the Cardinals' outfield for 13 seasons. He inspired countless youngsters to play the game the proper way—by hustling all of the time, advice he received as a minor-leaguer and never forgot.

Rob Rains

Enos Slaughter became the archetypical St. Louis Cardinal, his speed and hustle and daring virtually an organization symbol as much as that pair of proud redbirds.

Donald Honig

ENOS "COUNTRY" SLAUGHTER
Right field (1938–42, 1946–53)

The Cardinals' personification of all-out play, Slaughter was part of what many consider the finest outfield in Redbird annals, with left fielder Stan Musial and center fielder Terry Moore.

He is best known for his immortal "Mad Dash," the eighth-inning sprint from first base to home on Harry Walker's single to center that eventually proved to be the deciding run in the 1946 World Series Game 7 victory over the Boston Red Sox. In addition, Slaughter helped lead the Cards to a world championship in 1942.

The bald-headed but seemingly ageless Slaughter, even while losing three years to World War II duty, would play 19 major-league seasons, 13 with St. Louis. He was selected to the All-Star Game 10 times in Cardinal Red.

Bob Gibson—what a great competitor. Watching him in the clubhouse the day he was ready to pitch, nobody even made eye contact with him. I mean nobody. Not if you were smart. That was his day, and he was ready to pitch, and nobody better get in his way.

Bob Forsch

When I knocked a guy down, there was no second part to the story.

Bob Gibson

on batters retaliating after being hit by a pitch

Many longtime baseball observers agree that if there was one game they absolutely had to win, the pitcher they would want on the mound is Bob Gibson.

Rob Rains

Bob Gibson
Pitcher (1959–75)

The Stare with a Glare, Gibson more than any other player embodied the passion and spirit of the 1960s' twice-world-champion Cardinals. His high powerball froze batters, and his willingness to dust them made him the most feared pitcher of his time.

The Hall of Famer posted hypnotic numbers, the most impressive being the 1.12 ERA carved in 1968 for pitchers with more than 300 innings pitched—an epic milestone. His 17 strikeouts against Detroit in Game 1 of the 1968 World Series remains a Series record. In fact, seven Gibson marks are still World Series standards.

For his many achievements, Gibson has been honored as a two-time Cy Young Award winner, nine-time Gold Glove winner, league MVP, two-time World Series MVP, and nine-time National League All-Star.

Your players have to respect your knowledge. Be honest, be fair. But first, they have to know that you know what the hell to do.

Whitey Herzog

Where Whitey Herzog stood out from other managers was in his ability to predict moves in advance. He always knew if he made a pitching change what response the other team was going to make. He was able to anticipate matchups as far as a couple of innings in advance, and that let him always have his guys prepared and get the matchup that he wanted.

Red Schoendienst

WHITEY HERZOG
Manager (1980–90)

The fact that Herzog could talk to owner Gussie Busch in a manner Busch wouldn't tolerate from anyone else, ever, is an insight into the success and effectiveness of Whitey Herzog as a manager.

He spoke his mind and was listened to, but more than that, he was the consummate baseball strategist. Tony La Russa will pass him for second place in club annals for most wins behind Red Schoendienst early in the 2005 season and may well become the franchise's all-time winningest manager down the line.

But for now, Herzog, innovator of "Whiteyball" in the 1980s—that speed-steal-sacrifice-single brand of ball that was the trademark of his teams and yielded three National League pennants and one world title—cannot be headed.

CARDINALS ALL-TIME TEAM

Jim Bottomley, *first base*
Rogers Hornsby, *second base*
Ken Boyer, *third base*
Ozzie Smith, *shortstop*
Ted Simmons, *catcher*
Stan Musial, *left field*
Curt Flood, *center field*
Enos Slaughter, *right field*
Bob Gibson, *pitcher*
Whitey Herzog, *manager*

NATIONAL LEAGUE MVPS

1925	**Rogers Hornsby**	1946	**Stan Musial**
1926	**Bob O'Farrell**	1948	**Stan Musial**
1928	**Jim Bottomley**	1964	**Ken Boyer**
1931	**Frankie Frisch**	1967	**Orlando Cepeda**
1934	**Dizzy Dean**	1968	**Bob Gibson**
1937	**Joe Medwick**	1971	**Joe Torre**
1942	**Mort Cooper**	1979	**Keith Hernandez** *
1943	**Stan Musial**	1985	**Willie McGee**
1944	**Marty Marion**		*co-winner with Willie Stargell, Pittsburgh

NL ROOKIES OF THE YEAR

1954	**Wally Moon**, *outfield*	1985	**Vince Coleman**, *outfield*
1955	**Bill Virdon**, *outfield*	1986	**Todd Worrell**, *pitcher*
1974	**Bake McBride**, *outfield*	2001	**Albert Pujols**, *third base/outfield*

RETIRED CARDINALS NUMBERS

1   **Ozzie Smith**, shortstop (1982–96)
— *jersey retired: 1996*

2   **Red Schoendienst**, second base (1945–56, 1961–63) — *jersey retired: 1996*

6   **Stan Musial**, left field/right field/first base (1941–44, 1946–63) — *jersey retired: 1963*

9   **Enos Slaughter**, right field (1938–42, 1946–53)
— *jersey retired: 1996*

14   **Ken Boyer**, third base (1955–65)
— *jersey retired: 1984*

17   **Dizzy Dean**, pitcher (1930, 1932–37)
— *jersey retired: 1974*

20   **Lou Brock**, left field (1964–79)
— *jersey retired: 1979*

42   In honor of **Jackie Robinson**
— *jersey retired: 1997*

45   **Bob Gibson**, pitcher (1959–75)
— *jersey retired: 1975*

85   **August A. Busch Jr.**, (1953–89)
— *jersey retired: 1984*

(No #) **Rogers Hornsby**, second base (1915–26, 1933)
— *jersey retired: 1997*

(No #) **Jack Buck**, broadcaster (1954–59, 1961–2001)
— *jersey retired: 2002*

9

THE GREAT CARDINAL TEAMS

THE 1942 ST. LOUIS Cardinals are remembered by those who saw them as one of baseball's greatest all-time teams. The claim is not borne out by statistics, for the '42 Cardinals batted a modest .268 (best in the league) and hit just 60 home runs. What was remarkable was their unity. Few clubs have ever attacked with such élan or pure baseball sense. Virtually every man on the club had risen from the farm system. It was a young, hungry, daring team that refused to believe it could be beaten, and that, in the end, was not beaten, because they ran out every grounder, dove for every ball, and took every extra base.

Donald Honig

The Cardinals reached the 100-victory plateau for the first time in franchise history and became the first National League team to top the century mark in 18 years.

Rob Rains
on the 1931 world champions

Other Cardinal teams received more ink, but the 1931 club went on to defeat the powerful Philadelphia A's and keep Connie Mack from winning his third World Series in a row.

Bill Hallahan
pitcher (1925–26, 1929–36)

There's no question that the best club I ever played with was the happily efficient Cardinal team of 1931.

Frankie Frisch

I've seen a lot of great ball clubs in my day, but for pitching, hitting, spirit, and all-around balance, I would back my 1931 Cardinal team against any of them.

Gabby Street
manager (1929–33)

The '34 Cardinals were the best club I've ever been associated with. We fought amongst ourselves, yes, but God forbid if anybody picked a fight with us, because then they'd have to lick all 23 Cardinals.

Leo Durocher

How such a diverse collection of individuals coalesced as a great team is indeed mysterious. Some tried to explain it, but most were resigned to the fact that it was simply a group of people who hated to lose.

Doug Feldmann
on the 1934 Cardinals

In the wake of the Western dust blown up by the two cyclonic Deans, the St. Louis Cardinals take their place today on the top plateau of baseball.

Grantland Rice
*on the '34 Gas House Gang,
following their World Series
triumph over Detroit*

Putting on one of the most incredible finishes in baseball history, manager Billy Southworth's 1942 Cardinals won 41 of their final 48 games and stormed to the National League pennant. The Cards forged a first-place tie with the Dodgers less than a month after facing a $9^1/_2$-game deficit, then moved into first place—to stay—on September 13. St. Louis clinched the pennant on the final day of the season, completing a 20–4 September run. The Cardinals' 106 victories set a franchise record that still stands.

Rob Rains

Some people think the 1946 team was one of the greatest Cardinals clubs of all time, and it's hard to argue with them. Musial was the leader, of course, but the captain of the team was Terry Moore, the center fielder. Terry never raised his voice, but you knew he meant something when he said it. If he didn't think a guy had run fast enough to first base, he would walk up to him in the dugout and say, "You didn't run as fast as you can. Let's put out a little more." He didn't have to shout, he had that kind of control.

Red Schoendienst

The 1944 Cardinals were highlighted by a record-setting defense. Led by shortstop Marty Marion, the team's leader in the absence of Terry Moore, the Cardinals set a major-league record with a .982 fielding percentage.

Rob Rains

The 1946 World Series remains a dramatic high point in Cardinal history. The club had taken four pennants and three championships in five years and had assumed dynastic status.

Donald Honig

The 1964 season, one of the most exciting in Cardinals history, saw a major trade—the acquiring of Lou Brock; the firing of GM Bing Devine; and a comeback from a seemingly impossible $6^{1}/_{2}$-game margin with two weeks left to play to win the pennant, the first for the franchise since our title in 1946.

Red Schoendienst

The strength of the team lay in its ironman infield of Kenny Boyer at third, Dick Groat at shortstop, Julian Javier at second, and Bill White at first. That foursome averaged 160 games per person in 1963, and each had been an All Star.

Mel Freese

on the 1964 Redbirds

We would not have won the 1964 pennant had we not made the trade for Lou Brock, getting him from the Cubs in a six-player deal on the June 15 trading deadline in what turned out to be the greatest deal in Cardinal history.

Red Schoendienst

Orlando Cepeda gave the nickname of "El Birdos" to the Cardinals. He was one of the cheerleaders of the club. His nickname was "Cha Cha." Other nicknames included "Hoot" for Bob Gibson, "Bones" for Dal Maxvill, and "Creeper" for Larry Jaster. Julian Javier was "the Phantom," Roger Maris was "Rajah," Tim McCarver was "Doggie," and Mike Shannon was "Moon Man."

Mel Freese
on the 1967 world champions

One of the reasons why the Cardinals were in first place in late August 1967 was Roger Maris. While he hadn't hit like the Maris of old, at least for power, he was the leading clutch hitter in the league. He had more game-winning hits than any other player. He was also a team leader and a role model for younger players.

Mel Freese

The 1982 Cardinals ran at every opportunity, and they scooted all the way to a World Series championship. They often scored without the benefit of a hit, turning a walk, a stolen base, a ground ball, and a sacrifice fly into a rally. "Small ball" would ignite the Cardinals to three pennants in a six-year span.

Rob Rains

In 1982, Whitey's way turned out to be the winning way, giving us a team with more speed and that played better defense so we could take advantage of the dimensions of our own stadium. With Lonnie Smith as the catalyst, we put runners on the bases and generated a lot of excitement. The media even coined the phrase "Whiteyball" for the style of play. It was simple fundamental baseball, and it worked.

Red Schoendienst

The 1982 Cardinals hit just 67 home runs, leading Whitey Herzog to wonder at one point during the season whether the team would break Roger Maris's record.

Donald Honig

The "Whiteyball" Cards became the first division winner ever to finish last in the major leagues in home runs.

This is not the best Cardinals team ever. Our club in 1942 was better.

Stan Musial

on the 2004 National League champion Cardinals

The 1942 Cardinals trailed the Brooklyn Dodgers by 10 games with seven weeks to go. They won 43 of their final 51 games to win the pennant by two games.

Look at all the ways they [the 2004 Cardinals] can beat you. But don't forget that 1942 group. It still holds the franchise record for wins [106].

Mike Shannon

third baseman-outfielder (1962–70)/longtime Cardinals broadcaster

We had great teams in 1943 and '44, but I rank this current team [2004] behind our '42 club. This team has more power and good relief pitching. I do think this is the Cardinals' best offensive team ever.

Stan Musial

We [the 1942 Cardinals] never got down even when we were behind. This team [2004] does the same thing. Pujols, Rolen, Edmonds, Walker—those guys are great hitters.

Stan Musial

We got every element.

Larry Walker

*right fielder (2004–),
on the 2004 Cardinals after they
captured their 16th pennant, rally-ing from a 3–2 deficit against
the Houston Astros and Roger
Clemens in the 2004 NLCS*

FIELDS
OF PLAY

THE END OF ONE of baseball's historic stadiums came at 3:15 p.m. on May 8, 1966, when the Cardinals suffered a 10–5 defeat at the hands of the San Francisco Giants. Shortly after the game, a helicopter hovered over second base as home plate was unearthed and loaded into its cargo bin for transport to the shining new downtown stadium. Within a short time, the structure that contained nearly all of St. Louis's baseball history was razed.

Doug Feldmann

on Sportsman's Park (renamed Busch Stadium in 1953)

That first St. Louis National League club of 1876 played on the same field on which Terry Moore, Stan Musial, Whitey Kurowski, Marty Marion, and Mort Cooper romped and did their stuff.

Frederick G. Lieb

It was in 1892 that the Cardinals' lineage began. That team played its first season at Grand Avenue and Dodier Street, where numerous structures called Sportsman's Park would exist over the years. From 1893 through June 1920, the Cardinals played at Robison Field (Natural Bridge and Vandeventer avenues).

Rob Rains

Sportsman's Park had a foreboding feature. Around the outfield was a concrete wall, 11 feet high. Fly balls rebounded swiftly when not caught. If the outfielder ran full tilt against the wall—as Ray Blades of the Cardinals did, and Earle Combs and Pete Reiser of visiting clubs—careers could be ended or curtailed.

Bob Broeg

I recall how big it looked when we got there. Sportsman's Park. I remember the sights and sounds as though it were yesterday: the towering stands, the noise, the smell of popcorn, the vendors, the billboards, the flags, and the huge scoreboard.

Jim Shucart

Sportsman's Park was home to the Cardinals from July 1920 to May 1966.

NATIONAL BASEBALL HALL OF FAME LIBRARY, COOPERSTOWN, N.Y.

As with most ballparks of baseball's Golden Age, advertisements adorned much of the area behind the outfield at Sportsman's Park. Among the most evident of these was the famous billboard for Griesediecks' Beer, which for decades stared back at players and fans from the right-field wall.

Doug Feldmann

In the days at Sportsman's Park, there were only 15 to 20 lockers. Some of the extra ballplayers had to double up. For the marginal player or the green rookie there was a side room with a nail on the wall. Players like Musial and Marty Marion had to use that single nail when they first came up to join the Cardinals.

Bill Borst

Sportsman's was truly a neighborhood ballpark, the essence of which in contemporary times is seen only at the intersection of Addison and Clark streets in Chicago.

Doug Feldmann

Outside the northeast section at Busch Stadium stands a tall bronze statue of Stan Musial. It has become the meeting place of countless fans.

Rob Rains

St. Louis's "second" Busch Stadium was inaugurated in May 1966.

Every time I go to Busch Stadium, I still get a sense that I am part of a large extended family.

Stan Musial

If one attends a Cardinals-Cubs game at Busch Stadium or Wrigley Field, an equal throng of Chicago and St. Louis supporters will be found at each venue.

Doug Feldmann

The Cardinals played their first home game at Busch Stadium on May 12, 1966.

I was in Busch Stadium to see Bob Gibson's 3,000th strikeout, Ozzie Smith's playoff-winning home run in 1985, and Tom Lawless's homer against the Twins in 1987. My dad tells me I saw games at Sportsman's Park, but all I ever did was play with the seats.

Jim Grillo

fan

It sure holds the heat well.

Casey Stengel

New York Mets manager,
on Busch Stadium, after the 1966
All-Star Game

THE CUBS RIVALRY

Blue and red can be matching colors. But Cubbie blue and Cardinals red seem diametrically opposite.

George Castle and Jim Rygelski

Cubs-Cards games have been emotional—and historic. Stan Musial collected his 3,000th career hit at Wrigley Field. Lou Brock's 3,000th bounded off the hand of the Cubs' Dennis Lamp at Busch Stadium. Mark McGwire's record-breaking 62nd homer was against Chicago's Steve Trachsel at Busch.

Rob Rains

There is no greater rivalry in sports than the Cardinals and the Cubs, and it doesn't matter if the game is at Busch Stadium or at Wrigley Field. Fans from both teams will pack the place, and it will be jumping.

Stan Musial

Between games of a 1922 Chicago-St. Louis doubleheader, the clubs swapped outfielders. Cliff Heathcote played for the Cardinals in the first game and was in the Cubs' lineup in the night-cap. Max Flack was a Cub in the opener, a Cardinal in the second game.

Rob Rains

When I was a boy, I learned that one of the ways to have more fun rooting for my team was to have another team to hate with a passion. For me, that team was the Chicago Cubs.

Jim Grillo

Neither side could tell you that the Cubs were making a big mistake when they traded Lou Brock to the Cardinals in a six-player deal in 1964, with pitcher Ernie Broglio the principal player going to Chicago. Brock turned into a Hall of Famer, and Broglio hurt his arm and won only seven games for the Cubs in three years. Fans of both teams reflect on the deal as fate—the kind that more often than not has favored the Cardinals.

Rob Rains

Maybe because Stan Musial was my idol, I tried harder in the games I played against him.

Ernie Banks
"Mr. Cub," when asked why he played consistently well against St. Louis

There were epic pitching duels between Hall of Famers Bob Gibson and Ferguson Jenkins. Bruce Sutter and Lee Smith saved games for both teams, and Rogers Hornsby showed his extraordinary batting prowess both as a Cardinal and a Cub. Harry Caray was a legend in both broadcasting booths.

Rob Rains

I knew if I was pitching against [Bob] Gibson, runs would be at a minimum. If I gave up two or three runs, I was a loser.

Ferguson Jenkins

pitcher, Chicago Cubs (1966–73, 1982–83)

Jenkins once rated Gibson the toughest competitor he had ever faced.

The Cubs-Cardinals rivalry was a big part of my career. It made you reach a little higher when you played the Cardinals. The games almost always were exciting. They'd score three in the first, you'd score one, but somehow the game ended up tied in the eighth.

Billy Williams

Cubs Hall of Fame left fielder

Cardinals fans still bemoan that June day in 1984, when Ryne Sandberg hit two home runs off Bruce Sutter—one that tied the game in the ninth inning and another that deadlocked it in the 10th. Almost no one remembers that St. Louis's Willie McGee hit for the cycle in the same game, which the Cubs won in 11 innings.

Rob Rains

It's just a great rivalry, not a blood-type rivalry. It's a fierce rivalry. Each team wants to win badly. But there's respect. You go into Chicago, the fans are great. They're on you, but on you in good nature. You do something good, they respect it. You do something bad, they boo you.

Willie McGee

center fielder (1982–90, 1996–99)

From what I understand before I moved over from Oakland, they've had the best rivalries in the game. Every time we go into Wrigley Field, every time people come into Busch Stadium, when we play each other, it's a great game. People get up for it. I don't know if it had anything to do with myself and Sammy (Sosa).

Mark McGwire

It was one of the friendliest personal rivalries ever seen in sports, an example of sportsmanship rarely seen in today's dog-eat-dog world.

**George Castle and
Jim Rygelski**
*on the Mark McGwire-Sammy
Sosa home run race of 1998*

I was a Cubs fan in 1945. Then things kind of deteriorated with the team. Call it hero worship—I liked Stan Musial. He was in his prime then. I kind of swung over.

James Hage
Plano, Illinois, dentist

12

CARDINAL FANS

FANS HAVE CHEERED JOSE Oquendo and Rex Hudler and Joe McEwing, not because they were great players, but because they played the game at warp speed, diving for balls, sliding headfirst.

Rob Rains

Everything here seems to come full circle back to the ballpark. I feel I'm part of, well, a common cause.

Ozzie Smith

Because of their understanding and appreciation of the game, St. Louis fans cheer the deeds of both superstars and bench players. When third-string catcher Glenn Brummer stole home in a game in 1982, it was a moment to cherish. It still is.

Rob Rains

The saddest day for me as a fan was when we sent Keith Hernandez to New York for Neil Allen. I cried when I heard the news. The next morning I went into a florist's shop. The lady ahead of me was purchasing a lush, mixed bouquet, which had been spray-painted black. I remarked about the flowers, and she told me they were meant as a humorous gift for a disconsolate Hernandez fan.

Tina Wright

There is something different about wearing a Cardinal uniform and the different expectations of the fans who follow those players.

Stan Musial

Tommy Herr was like a god to me when I was growing up. He wasn't the most prolific player on the team, but he had the heart to make things happen. While other kids were crazy over Ozzie and his backflips, I loved to watch Tommy bat, or complete a double play. I will only have one favorite of all time, and that is the man with little power but a big game: Tommy Herr.

T. J. Crawford

fan

Fans here in St. Louis respect people who just play hard and keep their mouths shut.

Bob Forsch

We had a routine: Each night, we'd get into my car, tune the radio to KMOX, and drive until the reception became clear.

Mark Rubin

fan,
who followed the 1987 pennant
race with college friends in Texas
also from the St. Louis area

When I moved to East Tennessee, I could only get KMOX on my car radio. How many nights I have spent sitting in my car to follow the games.

Jeff S. Kee

fan

Growing up as a Cardinal fan in a small town in southern Illinois, our radio was almost always set to KMOX, and Jack Buck's voice was as familiar as the voices of people I knew. If one walked outdoors, day or night, during the summer, Jack's voice could be heard coming from radios throughout the neighborhood.

Peggy Heilig
fan

We were lucky enough to take our three children to the last Friday Cardinals home game in 1998, in which McGwire hit home run Number 66. The ballpark had a World Series-like atmosphere that day.

Carol Beck
fan

I truly wanted to do it here, guys. Thank you, St. Louis.

Mark McGwire
to Cardinals fans at Busch Stadium, Sept. 8, 1998, after breaking Roger Maris's 37-year-old major-league record for most home runs in a single season with his 62nd home run

I think it's harder to be a fan today, because of the lack of continuity of players. Years ago, fans not only knew the players on their teams but often knew all of the opposing teams' rosters as well. That's almost impossible now, and I think this change has hurt the game. Nonetheless, baseball will always be my sport, and the Redbirds will always be my team.

Peggy Heilig

The fans will never know how important they are for every player, no matter the sport.

Red Schoendienst

I take my glove to the game, but I haven't gotten a foul ball. I carry it in my van almost everywhere I go. To tell the truth, I'd rather watch it on television. The beer's cheaper, and the restrooms aren't crowded.

Clarence Vollmar

77-year-old fan and memorabilia collector, Florissant, Mo., in 2003

13

CARDINAL SINS

IF I WAS PLAYING third base, and my mother was rounding third with the winning run, I'd trip her. Oh, I'd pick her up, dust her off, and say, "Sorry, Mom," but nobody beats me.

Leo Durocher

Medwick and Terry Moore had been playing alongside each other in the Cardinals outfield for six years when a ball was hit high and deep into left center. As Terry went charging toward the fence in pursuit, he relied on Medwick to warn him if he were in any danger. Medwick was hollering that Moore had plenty of room as the ball sailed 20 feet into the stands. Terry crashed into the concrete wall. When he came to, Moore told Medwick that if he ever ran him into the fence again, he'd break his neck.

Enos Slaughter

I watched the crowd and Medwick and the pelting missiles through my field glasses. It was a terrifying sight. Every face in the crowd, women and men, was distorted by rage. Mouths were torn wide open, eyes glistened in the sun. All fists were clenched. Only the barrier of a steel screen and locked gates prevented them from pouring onto the field and mobbing Medwick.

Paul Gallico

legendary sports journalist, on Tigers fans' reaction to Ducky Medwick's aggressive slide into Detroit third baseman Marv Owen after his run-scoring triple in the top of the sixth inning of Game 7 of the 1934 World Series. Upon taking his position in left field in the bottom of the inning, fruit, vegetables, and other objects rained on Medwick. Commissioner Kenesaw Mountain Landis, after conferring with both players, ordered Medwick's removal from the game for his safety

I don't know where they were getting all that stuff from. It was like they were backing produce trucks up to the gate and supplying everybody.

Charlie Gehringer

*Detroit Tigers Hall of Fame
second baseman,
on the Medwick incident in
Game 7 of the 1934 World Series,
at Navin Field. The brouhaha
delayed the game for 17 minutes*

It cut my heart out. I cried like a baby. I'd been a Cardinal since 1935, and I don't think anybody who's ever worn a Cardinal uniform was ever more loyal to it than I was or put out as hard as I did. But you go. You have to.

Enos "Country" Slaughter

*on his trade to the New York
Yankees before the 1954 season,
after 13 years in St. Louis*

Yesterday we saw what was probably the greatest managerial World Series boner in the history of baseball. Frankie Frisch took a million-dollar asset and used him on a ten-cent job. . . . In the press box reporters looked at one another, puzzled. Dean to run? What for? The batboy can run.

Paul Gallico

on Dizzy Dean's near-suicidal pinch-running gaffe in Game 4 of the 1934 World Series against Detroit, in which the Cardinals' mound ace got nailed in the head by a relay throw to first base in the fourth inning. Before Cards manager Frankie Frisch had decided on a pinch runner for Spud Davis, who had just singled, Dean jumped up and sprinted out to first base as the replacement. Frisch shrugged and let it stand, then of course was second-guessed moments later

You can't hurt no Dean by hittin' him on the head.

Dizzy Dean

following the pinch-run beaning. After spending the night in the hospital, Dean, miraculously, started the next day's Game 5, pitching into the ninth inning but dropping a 3–1 decision

In 1970 Steve Carlton dropped to 10–19, leading the league in losses, thus joining a curious circle—great pitchers who led the league in defeats, their numbers including Phil Niekro, Paul Derringer, Red Ruffing, and Robin Roberts, among others.

Donald Honig

I don't care if he ever throws another damn ball for us.

August Busch Jr.
owner (1953–89),
on pitcher Steve Carlton
(1965–71)

In 1970, Carlton held out for a three-year $50,000 contract, then went out and logged a deplorable 10–19 season record. After posting an impressive turnaround 20–9 mark in 1971, Carlton raised his ante to $75,000, but Busch had had enough, trading the talented southpaw to Philadelphia, where he became a four-time Cy Young Award winner and Hall of Fame pitcher.

The greatest loss was the trade of Steve Carlton to Philadelphia. He won a career total of 329 games. Only Warren Spahn won more as a left-hander. Carlton had 77 Cardinal wins when traded. Net result: It probably cost the Cardinals three or four division titles in the 1970s.

Mel Freese

He needed his hair, like the Biblical Sampson, for his pitching power. To shore him of his hair was to strip him of his psychological edge on the mound. Hrabosky delighted crowds in every city with his "mad routine." He constantly stepped off the mound to "psych" himself to an intense state before delivering his next pitch. Without his hair, Hrabosky was just another mediocre pitcher whose fastball tended to rise en route to the upper deck.

Bill Borst

on "the Mad Hungarian," Al Hrabosky. Then-Cardinals manager Vern Rapp had instituted a hair-length and clean-shaven policy for players during his tenure (1977–78)

You simply cannot let the bleacher creatures get under your skin. Those players who do, end up flipping the bird at the fans. But Jim "Mudcat" Grant went further—he threw strikes at them.

George Castle and
Jim Rygelski

on the unraveling of Cardinals pitcher Grant on June 29, 1969, at Wrigley Field. Beset by Cubs fans before the game while in the bullpen, Grant suddenly went ballistic on the crowd, throwing six 90-mile-an-hour fastballs attempting to hit an adult heckler. Grant instead wound up nailing an 11-year-old boy in the neck, a young girl in the jaw, and a third kid in the arm. Surprisingly, no punitive action was taken by the National League against Grant

Don't count your wins until you've won. This lesson was driven into the Cardinals' minds on July 18, 1994, in Houston. St. Louis, ahead 11–0 after three innings, saw the Astros come back to win the game, 15–12.

Rob Rains

What do I wanna do that for? They go out to 50 people and I'm supposed to stop what I'm doing for them?

Whitey Herzog
complaining in 1980 about the fledgling cable-only ESPN sports network asking to interview him

14

THE
LOCKER ROOM

Every day a Cardinals player walks into that locker room and puts on the birds-on-the-bat jersey, they should realize how lucky they are and say a special thank-you to whoever was responsible for them being there.

Stan Musial

I'm as nauseous as I've ever been. I have a terrible headache. My head is pounding. I feel like throwing up and I'm having trouble swallowing. And the beauty of it is, you want to feel like this every day.

Tony La Russa

during the 1996 NL Central Division title race with his team in contention

Dizzy Dean said that Paul Waner was the toughest hitter he ever faced, and that Lloyd Waner was much the same.

Doug Feldmann

When Mike Laga hit a foul ball out of Busch Stadium in 1986—no batted ball of any kind had ever left the stadium's confines—there was a buzz in the crowd. Fans realized they had just witnessed a first.

Rob Rains

Laga, a utility first baseman, played for St. Louis from 1986 through 1988.

I'm not a dignified man myself, but when I look back over the [1931] World Series between the Cardinals and Athletics, I always remember how the fans booed President Herbert Hoover in the first game at Philadelphia. They cheered me —me, a rookie from Oklahoma who could run a little—and booed the president of the United States.

Pepper Martin

One of the key players in helping to create the culture of the new Cardinal clubhouse was a man few people knew. George "Big Daddy" Crowe was gone from the team by 1964, but he played a vital role in bridging the gap from one era to another. If you were casting him in a movie, the writer Robert Boyle once said, you would want the young James Earl Jones. His silences had as much meaning as his words. In another era, Crowe might well have been a manager or even a general manager. No one was going to abuse anyone or bully anyone on a team as long as George Crowe was there. And no one was going to toss racial epithets around lightly. Almost unconsciously, he merged the cultures of the two races.

David Halberstam
author

Someone I got to know that I remained friends with was Gene Autry. The Singing Cowboy had always been a Cardinals fan.

Enos Slaughter

Dizzy Dean once walked a hitter with two out in the ninth inning so he could pitch to Bill Terry. He walked in from the mound and told Terry he had promised some hospitalized kids he would strike out Terry that day. He did too.

Rob Rains

Music would come from Pepper's "Mudcat Band," which featured Martin on harmonica and guitar, Lon Warneke on guitar, left-hander Bob Weiland blowing into a cloudy jug, outfielder Frenchy Bordagaray on a setup that included a washboard, whistle, and automobile horn, and pitcher Bill McGee on a broken-down fiddle (it earned him the nickname "Fiddler Bill"). They played semblances of cowboy and hillbilly tunes, and they sang and cavorted and wore outlandish outfits (including a grass skirt for Pepper). While Frisch lamented that he was "the only manager who travels with is own orchestra."

Donald Honig

circa 1937–38

A clattering Spike Jones novelty song, "Pass the Biscuits, Mirandy," soon became the team's victory song. It was played and sung after each win. The trainer, Dr. Harrison J. Weaver, played the mandolin, and Stan Musial handled a slide whistle or kept time with coathanger drumsticks. A new Cardinal band was being formed which would lead the parade down the stretch drive.

Mel Freese

during the 1942 season

The fastest man I ever saw getting showered and dressed after a game was Enos Slaughter. In the time it took me to unfasten the shoelaces on my spikes, he had showered, dressed, and left the ballpark.

Red Schoendienst

Baseball used to be a newspaper game. You had to wait until you picked up the morning newspaper to find out the scores of the other games from the previous day, looking at the standings to find out if you had gained ground or lost a game. The influence of television has changed the way writers for newspapers cover baseball. It has put them into a different role and has changed the relationship many players used to have with writers. They weren't the enemy to us, they were friends, and there wasn't the separation between the two sides that seems to exist today.

Red Schoendienst

Everybody thinks of baseball as a sacred cow. When you have the verve to challenge it, people look down their noses at you. There are a lot of things wrong with a lot of industries . . . baseball is one of them.

Curt Flood
center field (1958–69)

The 1967 Cardinals had a mixture of white, black, and Hispanic players. Bob Gibson called the Cardinals the "Rainbow Coalition" long before Jesse Jackson ever coined the phrase.

Mel Freese

Lou Brock is one of 25 players in major-league history to collect 3,000 hits in his career, but one of only eight who never won a league batting title.

Rob Rains

To loosen up the clubhouse, trainer Gene Gieselmann played the old "mongoose trick" on rookie Willie McGee. He placed a box labeled "wild mongoose" by McGee's locker. When McGee opened it, out popped a fake furry critter. McGee was last seen trying to climb atop a locker.

Mel Freese

Three Cardinals—Red Schoendienst, Reggie Smith, and Ted Simmons—each hit home runs from both sides of the plate in one game.

Rob Rains

The secret of success lies in knowing your men—and when to take out your pitcher.

Frankie Frisch

I heard he could hit.

Bob Gibson

when asked why he once hit John Milner with a pitch

15

CARDINALS
WORLD CHAMPION
ROSTERS

Six Cardinals have played *in four World Series (Bottomley, Frisch, Chick Hafey, Kurowski, Marion, and Musial), while Lou Brock is the Redbirds' Mr. October, leading in seven of the club's 12 major batting categories for World Series play, including home runs, hits, RBIs, stolen bases, and runs. Bob Gibson has been St. Louis's money pitcher in the Fall Classic, posting top performances in seven of the Cardinals' top 10 World Series pitching categories, including most wins, strikeouts, complete games, and fewest walks.*

1926
89–65
*World Series victors
over New York Yankees, 4–3*

Rogers Hornsby, *manager*

Grover Cleveland Alexander, *pitcher*
Hi Bell, *pitcher*
Les Bell, *third base*
Jim Bottomley, *first base*
Taylor Douthit, *center field*
Jake Flowers, *pinch hitter*
Chick Hafey, *left field*
Jesse Haines, *pitcher*
Bill Hallahan, *pitcher*
Wattie Holm, *outfield*
Rogers Hornsby, *second base*
Vic Keen, *pitcher*
Bob O'Farrell, *catcher*
Art Reinhart, *pitcher*
Flint Rehm, *pitcher*
Bill Sherdel, *pitcher*
Billy Southworth, *right field*
Tommy Thevenow, *shortstop*
Specs Toporcer, *pinch hitter*

Starting lineups in bold

1931

101–53

*World Series victors
over Philadelphia Athletics, 4–3*

Gabby Street, *manager*

Sparky Adams, *third base*
Ray Blades, *pinch hitter*
Jim Bottomley, *first base*
Ripper Collins, *pinch hitter*
Paul Derringer, *pitcher*
Jake Flowers, *third base*
Frankie Frisch, *second base*
Charlie Gelbert, *shortstop*
Burleigh Grimes, *pitcher*
Chick Hafey, *left field*
Bill Hallahan, *pitcher*
Andy High, *third base*
Syl Johnson, *pitcher*
Jim Lindsey, *pitcher*
Gus Mancuso, *catcher*
Pepper Martin, *center field*
Ernie Orsatti, *outfield*
Flint Rhem, *pitcher*
Wally Roettger, *outfield*
George Watkins, *right field*
Jimmie Wilson, *catcher*

1934
95–58
*World Series victors
over Detroit Tigers, 4–3*

Frankie Frisch, *manager*

Tex Carleton, *pitcher*
Ripper Collins, *first base*
Pat Crawford, *pinch hitter*
Spud Davis, *catcher*
Dizzy Dean, *pitcher*
Paul Dean, *pitcher*
Bill DeLancey, *catcher*
Leo Durocher, *shortstop*
Frankie Frisch, *second base*
Chick Fullis, *outfield*
Jesse Haines, *pitcher*
Bill Hallahan, *pitcher*
Pepper Martin, *third base*
Joe "Ducky" Medwick, *left field*
Jim Mooney, *pitcher*
Ernie Orsatti, *center field*
Jack Rothrock, *right field*
Dazzy Vance, *pitcher*
Bill Walker, *pitcher*
Burgess Whitehead, *shortstop*

1942
106–48
*World Series victors
over New York Yankees, 4–1*

Billy Southworth, *manager*

Johnny Beazley, *pitcher*
Jimmy Brown, *second base*
Mort Cooper, *pitcher*
Walker Cooper, *catcher*
Creepy Crespi, *pinch runner*
Harry Gumbert, *pitcher*
Johnny Hopp, *first base*
Whitey Kurowski, *third base*
Max Lanier, *pitcher*
Marty Marion, *shortstop*
Terry Moore, *center field*
Stan Musial, *left field*
Ken O'Dea, *pinch hitter*
Howie Pollet, *pitcher*
Ray Sanders, *pinch hitter*
Enos "Country" Slaughter, *right field*
Harry Walker, *pinch hitter*
Ernie White, *pitcher*

1944
105–49
World Series victors
over St. Louis Browns, 4–2

Billy Southworth, *manager*

Augie Bergamo, *outfield*
Harry Brecheen, *pitcher*
Bud Byerly, *pitcher*
Mort Cooper, *pitcher*
Walker Cooper, *catcher*
Blix Donnelly, *pitcher*
George Fallen, *second base*
Debs Garms, *pinch hitter*
Johnny Hopp, *center field*
Al Jurisich, *pitcher*
Whitey Kurowski, *third base*
Max Lanier, *pitcher*
Danny Litwhiler, *left field*
Marty Marion, *shortstop*
Stan Musial, *right field*
Ken O'Dea, *pinch hitter*
Ray Sanders, *first base*
Freddy Schmidt, *pitcher*
Emil Verban, *second base*
Ted Wilks, *pitcher*

1946
98–58

*World Series victors
over Boston Red Sox, 4–3*

Eddie Dyer, *manager*

Johnny Beazley, *pitcher*
Alpha Brazle, *pitcher*
Harry Brecheen, *pitcher*
Murry Dickson, *pitcher*
Erv Dusak, *outfield*
Joe Garagiola, *catcher*
Nippy Jones, *pinch hitter*
Whitey Kurowski, *third base*
Marty Marion, *shortstop*
Terry Moore, *center field*
Red Munger, *pitcher*
Stan Musial, *first base*
Howie Pollet, *pitcher*
Del Rice, *catcher*
Red Schoendienst, *second base*
Dick Sisler, *pinch hitter*
Enos "Country" Slaughter, *right field*
Harry Walker, *left field*
Ted Wilks, *pitcher*

1964

93–69

*World Series victors
over New York Yankees, 4–3*

Johnny Keane, *manager*

Ken Boyer, *third base*
Lou Brock, *left field*
Gerry Buchek, *second base*
Roger Craig, *pitcher*
Curt Flood, *center field*
Bob Gibson, *pitcher*
Dick Groat, *shortstop*
Bob Humphreys, *pitcher*
Charlie James, *pinch hitter*
Julian Javier, *second base*
Dal Maxvill, *second base*
Tim McCarver, *catcher*
Gordie Richardson, *pitcher*
Ray Sadecki, *pitcher*
Barney Schultz, *pitcher*
Mike Shannon, *right field*
Curt Simmons, *pitcher*
Bob Skinner, *pinch hitter*
Ron Taylor, *pitcher*
Carl Warwick, *pinch hitter*
Bill White, *first base*

1967
101–60
*World Series victors
over Boston Red Sox, 4–3*

Red Schoendienst, *manager*

Eddie Bressoud, *shortstop*
Nelson Briles, *pitcher*
Lou Brock, *left field*
Steve Carlton, *pitcher*
Orlando Cepeda, *first base*
Curt Flood, *center field*
Phil Gagliano, *pinch hitter*
Bob Gibson, *pitcher*
Joe Hoerner, *pitcher*
Dick Hughes, *pitcher*
Larry Jaster, *pitcher*
Julian Javier, *second base*
Jack Lamabe, *pitcher*
Roger Maris, *right field*
Dal Maxvill, *shortstop*
Tim McCarver, *catcher*
Dave Ricketts, *pinch hitter*
Mike Shannon, *third base*
Ed Spiezio, *pinch hitter*
Bobby Tolan, *pinch hitter*
Ray Washburn, *pitcher*
Ron Willis, *pitcher*
Hal Woodeschick, *pitcher*

1982

92–70

*World Series victors
over Milwaukee Brewers, 4–3)*

Whitey Herzog, *manager*

Joaquin Andujar, *pitcher*
Doug Bair, *pitcher*
Steve Braun, *pinch hitter/outfield*
Glenn Brummer, *catcher*
Bob Forsch, *pitcher*
David Green, *outfield*
George Hendrick, *right field*
Keith Hernandez, *first base*
Tommy Herr, *second base*
Dane Iorg, *outfield*
Jim Kaat, *pitcher*
Jeff Lahti, *pitcher*
Dave LaPoint, *pitcher*
Willie McGee, *center field*
Ken Oberkfell, *third base*
Darrell Porter, *catcher*
Mike Ramsey, *third base*
Lonnie Smith, *left field*
Ozzie Smith, *shortstop*
John Stuper, *pitcher*
Bruce Sutter, *pitcher*
Gene Tenace, *catcher*

BIBLIOGRAPHY

Allen, Maury. *Baseball's 100: A Personal Ranking of the Best Players in Baseball History*. New York: Galahad Books, 1981.

Bodley, Hal. "Cards draw comparisons to 1942 world champs." *USA Today*, 15 October 2004: 5C.

Borst, Bill. *Baseball Through a Knothole: A St. Louis History*. St. Louis: Krank Press, 1980.

Borst, Bill. *The Best of Seasons: The 1944 St. Louis Cardinals and St. Louis Browns*. Jefferson, N.C.: McFarland & Company, Inc., Publishers, 1995.

Broeg, Bob. *Redbirds: A Century of Cardinals Baseball*. Marceline, Mo.: Walsworth Publishing Co., 1992.

Broeg, Bob and Jerry Vickery. *The St. Louis Cardinals Encyclopedia*. Lincolnwood, Ill.: Contemporary Books, 1998.

Broeg, Bob. "A Sportsman's Park." *Athlon Baseball*, 1994: 41.

Buck, Jack with Rob Rains, Bob Broeg. *Jack Buck: "That's a Winner!"* Champaign, Ill.: Sagamore Publishing, 1997.

Castle, George and Jim Rygelski. *The I-55 Series: Cubs vs. Cardinals*. Champaign, Ill.: Sports Publishing Inc., 1999.

Bibliography

Chadwick, Bruce and David M. Spindel. *The St. Louis Cardinals: Memories and Memorabilia from a Century of Baseball.* New York: Abbeville Press, 1995.

Chieger, Bob. *Voices of Baseball: Quotations on the Summer Game.* New York: Atheneum, 1983.

Devaney, John. *The Greatest Cardinals of Them All.* New York: G.P. Putnam's Sons, 1968.

Devaney, John. *Where Are They Today? Great Sports Stars of Yesteryear.* New York: Crown Publishers, Inc., 1985.

Dodd, Mike. "Rolen ends slump with two homers." *USA Today,* 15 October 2004: 5C.

Feldmann, Doug. *Dizzy and the Gas House Gang: The 1934 St. Louis Cardinals and Depression-Era Baseball.* Jefferson, N.C.: McFarland and Company, Inc., 2000.

Foley, Red and Topps Chewing Gum, Inc. *Topps Baseball Cards: St. Louis Cardinals.* Los Angeles: Price Stern Sloan, 1989.

Forsch, Bob with Tom Wheatley. *Bob Forsch's Tales from the Cardinals Dugout.* Champaign, Ill.: Sports Publishing L.L.C., 2003.

Freese, Mel. *The Glory Years of the St. Louis Cardinals, Vol. I: The World Championship Seasons.* St. Louis: Palmerston & Reed Publishing Co., 1999.

Golenbock, Peter. *The Spirit of St. Louis: A History of the St. Louis Cardinals and Browns.* New York: HarperCollins Publishers, Inc., 2000.

Graves, Gary. "Cards pull together; Pujols leads way." *USA Today,* 22 October 2004: 5C.

Graves, Gary. "Nixon gives Red Sox the cushion to relax." *USA Today,* 28 October 2004: 6C.

Halberstam, David. *October 1964.* New York: Fawcett Columbine, 1994.

Heinz, W. C. "Stan Musial's Last Day." *Best Sports Stories: A Panorama of the 1963 Sports Year.* Irving T. Marsh, Edward Ehre, Eds. New York: E. P. Dutton & Co., Inc., 1964. 70–78.

Honig, Donald. *The St. Louis Cardinals: An Illustrated History.* New York: Prentice Hall Press, 1991.

Hood, Robert E. *The Gashouse Gang.* New York: William Morrow and Company, Inc., 1976.

Johnson, Chuck. "Cardinals rule in NL." *USA Today,* 22 October 2004: 1C.

Kavanagh, Jack. *Baseball Legends: Dizzy Dean.* New York: Chelsea House Publishers, 1991.

Lieb, Frederick G. *The St. Louis Cardinals: The Story of a Great Baseball Club.* Carbondale, Ill.: Southern Illinois University Press, 2001.

McCarver, Tim with Phil Pepe. *Few and Chosen: Defining Cardinal Greatness Across the Eras.* Chicago: Triumph Books, 2003.

Rains, Rob. *Cardinal Nation.* St. Louis: *The Sporting News,* 2002.

Rains, Rob. *The Cardinals Fan's Little Book of Wisdom.* South Bend, Ind.: Diamond Communications, Inc., 1994.

Ross, Alan. *Echoes from the Ball Park.* Nashville, Tenn.: Walnut Grove Press, 1999.

Schoendienst, Red with Rob Rains. *Red.* Champaign, Ill.: Sports Publishing, 1998.

Slaughter, Enos with Kevin Reid. *Country Hardball: The Autobiography of Enos "Country" Slaughter.* Greensboro, N.C.: Tudor Publishers, Inc., 1991.

Smith, Curt. *America's Dizzy Dean.* St. Louis: The Bethany Press, 1978.

Thorn, John et al. *Total Baseball: The Official Encyclopedia of Major League Baseball*, Fifth Edition. New York: Viking Penguin, 1997.

Tiemann, Robert L. *Cardinal Classics: Outstanding Games from Each of the St. Louis Baseball Club's 100 Seasons 1882–1981.* St. Louis: Baseball Histories, Inc., 1982.

Vecsey, George. "Happy Days Are Here Again." *The Way It Was.* Ed. George Vecsey. New York: McGraw-Hill Book Company, 1974.

Wolfe, Rich. *For Cardinals Fans Only.* Phoenix, Ariz.: Lone Wolfe Press, 2003.

Wright, Tina, edit. *Cardinal Memories: Recollections from Baseball's Greatest Fans.* Columbia, Missouri: University of Missouri Press, 2000.

Young, James V. and Arthur F. McClure. *Remembering Their Glory: Sports Heroes of the 1940s.* Cranbury, N.J.: A.S. Barnes and Co., Inc., 1977.

WEBSITES:

www.netshrine.com/vbulletin2/showthread.php?t=4887&page=3&pp=15 (Ted Simmons)

www.espn.com, Oct. 14, 2004 (Pujols, Rolen)

INDEX

Index

Index

Index

Index

Index